REVIEW GUIDI
AND
LECTURE COMPANION

Larry Elowitz
Georgia College and State University

Government by the People

BASIC VERSION
2003-2004 Edition

James MacGregor Burns
University of Maryland, College Park and Williams College

J.W. Peltason
University of California

Thomas E. Cronin
Whitman College

David B. Magleby
Brigham Young University

David O'Brien
University of Virginia

Paul C. Light
New York University
Brookings Institute

Upper Saddle River, New Jersey 07458

© 2004 by PEARSON EDUCATION, INC.
Upper Saddle River, New Jersey 07458

ISBN 0-13-110182-X

Printed in the United States of America

Basic Version
Review Guide and Lecture Companion
Table of Contents

PREFACE

The basic goal of this new edition of the Study Guide to **GOVERNMENT BY THE PEOPLE** is that of its predecessors—to offer the reader a rational way to learn about American Government. To that end, the Guide covers the most significant aspects of each text chapter. In the final analysis, all true education is self-education. Students can claim no concept as their own until they can use it. Hopefully, the learning process can be shortened through students becoming their own tutors.

A long-term debt is owed to those students and teachers who have taken the time to comment on the strengths and weaknesses of this Study Guide since it was first published in 1963. But obviously, the greatest indebtedness is to James MacGregor Burns of Williams College; J.W. Peltason, University of California System; Thomas E. Cronin, Whitman College; David B. Magleby, Brigham Young University; and David O'Brien, University of Virginia. Their lively, insightful approach to American Government is the basis of this Study Guide. **GOVERNMENT BY THE PEOPLE** is in its fifth decade with the 2003-2004 edition still displaying all of its original zest.

Larry Elowitz, Georgia College and State University
Milledgeville, GA

How to Use the Companion Website

Both faculty and students will find the massive Companion Website for *Government by the People* to be enormously helpful. The website contains a robust range of features that will help the instructor to plan, manage, and implement a better, more interesting course and will assist students in their learning experience, by keeping their interest piqued and by offering to them a variety of helpful supplements.

For the instructor, the Companion Website under its "syllabus manager" facility offers a number of aids in planning your course.

- There is a sample course syllabus to show you what can be done with the website. The publisher provides a server on which you can place your syllabus so that students can have access to it at all times by going online. You would simply put the website address on the hard copy of your syllabus that you handed out in class. Students then would only have to type in the address once they had opened their browser. (If using their own computer, students would then likely bookmark the address, thus not having to type it in for each visit.) You can place assignments on your syllabus that would allow students to link to other websites, sites that are suggested at other places in the Companion Website. One useful feature of the sample syllabus is a calendar of the semester, with class dates highlighted. Students would click on the highlighted date to see the assignment for that date. You would have the ability to change the syllabus at your discretion by typing in your own ID and password. By taking advantage of the features provided by the publisher, your course syllabus would become a dynamic part of your course.
- The syllabus manager has a separate page for each chapter in *Government by the People*. Every chapter's page is organized in similar ways, providing a multitude of useful material for both the instructor and students.
- There is a list of faculty resources for each chapter. Included in the resources are Power Point images that can be downloaded for class use, a section providing lecture notes on current events (e.g., in light of the 2000 presidential election, should the Electoral College be abolished), a link to online teaching resources (such as the ASPAnet from the American Political Science Association Web page), and a comprehensive section on teaching strategies (that in effect gives the instructor guidance on every step in his/her career, from interviewing for a job to getting acquainted with colleagues to organizing for teaching to testing, and so on).
- Each chapter has a student resources section also, including state links (allowing the student to go the Web pages of each of the state governments), a career center (help in deciding on a major and a career), a writing guide (tips on how to write college essays), and further reading (other texts and articles keyed to each chapter).
- There are several identical elements in each chapter page. "Documents online" provides either the complete or a substantial portion of the text of dozens of major documents that are constantly referred to in this course and in the text. Examples include the Constitution, the Bill of Rights, *Brown v. Board of Education*, presidential debates, party platforms, and major bills such as the Americans with Disabilities Act and the Brady Bill. A section called "connect with politics" provides links to dozens of politically relevant groups, such as major media outlets, political

parties, advocacy groups, and government agencies. There is a political search engine that would allow students to click on major topics (such as the commerce clause) and then to link directly to one of the major Internet set engines (such as Yahoo!, Lycos, AltaVista, etc.) to find out what is available online on that subject. Also, students can choose to participate in a message board (sending inquiries to other users of the companion site throughout the country about where to find certain information) and a chat room (allowing, for example, students in your class to discuss class lectures or assigned topics). Moreover, each chapter page has links to other major sites, such as the *New York Times*, the U.S. Census Bureau, and to other specially produced supplements that will become available to keep the course tuned into current events.

- The chapter pages are organized in a standard format. First is a chapter overview, providing a quick summary of the major topics and graphics, and usually including a video that can be downloaded, and featuring one of the authors of the text summarizing a useful point. There is a section-by-section summary of the chapter's talking points. Then students are given a review, with questions in a variety of formats, including completion, multiple choice, true/false, essays, and glossary quizzes. Students can submit their answers for a grade. Students are also encouraged to take part in an opinion survey in each chapter that would allow them to see how they agree or disagree with the opinions of other users of the site. (Sample survey question: should the rights of minorities obstruct the will of the majority?) New to this edition of the text is a section called "PoliSim." Several chapters will have an interactive simulation that will allow the student to plan, for example, a strategy for a presidential candidate and to see the likely outcome in Electoral College votes, or to simulate a lobby group by researching Senators' voting records and then assigning "time" and "money" in an effort to get legislation passed; feedback includes seeing the probable consequences of the choice of tactics and resources.

From the instructor's viewpoint one of the more useful aspects of the Companion Website is the faculty resource section for each chapter. In addition to the lecture notes drawn from current events, there are images (i.e., photographs, diagrams, charts) and full PowerPoint slide shows that can be downloaded for your classroom use. After downloading, you can print the image or slides for photocopying and distribution to your class or for turning into transparencies. Increasingly, instructors are taking advantage of downloaded images to do their own classroom PowerPoint presentations. Each chapter has its own set of slides and images (including photographs, drawings, diagrams, and charts from the textbook).

Downloading the images is simple, once you get the hang of it—and getting the hang of it is truly easy. The images are located in each chapter's "faculty resources." The section is clearly labeled as PowerPoint slides. Left clicking (i.e., clicking with the left button) with your computer mouse on the PowerPoint icon will bring up the images of all of the photographs, diagrams, and other graphics available for that chapter. To download a particular image, right click (i.e., the right button on the mouse) once on that image. A menu box will open up with a variety of options. Select the option that reads "save picture as" or "save image as" and left click on that option. Another box will pop up asking you where and how to save the file. Type in a name for the file, make sure the file will be saved as a "gif" file (this should be the default option), and then choose a destination (i.e., folder) for the saved file. It would be a good idea to have created previously a folder on a disk and/or your hard drive for that chapter of the text, so that when you save a file you can store it in a clearly defined (and subsequently easily found) place on your computer. When you've saved one image, use the back button on your browser to go back to the page showing you all of the images and repeat the process, as you desire.

To prepare the image for a classroom PowerPoint slide presentation, you will need to open up your PowerPoint program and choose "blank presentation." Click on "insert" in the PowerPoint menu bar, select "picture," and then select "from file." A dialog box will pop up that will allow you to explore your computer's files; you will then need to find the folder into which you had previously stored the image. Once you have selected (i.e., clicked on) the file, choose the "insert" button to place the image into the blank presentation. Then save the presentation, again making sure you have saved it into a folder clearly named and easily found. Once saved on your hard drive and copied onto a floppy disk, you can then take that disk into your classroom, load it into the classroom's computer, and run a PowerPoint presentation show.

The textual slides are even easier to work with because they will be saved to your computer as a PowerPoint slide show, requiring no manipulation. Just left click on a particular chapter's PowerPoint slide show (also within the faculty resources section) and save to a folder on your computer. (Don't forget the points above about saving to clearly defined folders.) Then open up your PowerPoint program, find the folder and the file and open it. Voila! There will be a complete slide show tailored to that chapter. For example, the interest group chapter will have slides on types of interest groups, interest group tactics, factors shaping strength, and so on. Some instructors will photocopy the slides for classroom distribution, others will turn them into transparencies, and those with access to electronic classrooms will use them as PowerPoint classroom presentations.

One can even add images to the PowerPoint slide show. The simplest way would be, once you have downloaded a chapter's slide show and opened it on your computer, to add a slide to the slide show. Click on "insert" in the PowerPoint menu bar, choose "new slide" from the dialog box, select the blank presentation, and then insert the image exactly as described above in the section on images.

The process is not nearly as complicated as it sounds. After you've done it once or twice, it'll be old hat and you'll feel increasingly comfortable with the process. At any rate, you will find the Companion Website to be a major help to you and your students as you explore collectively contemporary American politics. The site address is www.prenhall.com/burns. Click on the cover of the 2003-2004 edition.

Dr. Larry Elowitz, Georgia College & State University

Chapter 1
Constitutional Democracy

PART I — GUIDEPOSTS

1. Introduction: The Challenge of September 11, 2001
    a. How did 9/11/01 challenge the American political system?
    b. What were typical pre-9/11 political attitudes?
    c. How did 9/11 renew the liberty-security debate?

2. American Government and Politicians in Context
    a. Why does democracy require a segment of the public to be attentive and informed?
    b. How does democracy relate to tolerance, faith in humanity, and realism about politicians?

3. Defining Democracy
    a. What is a constitutional democracy?
    b. How are these democratic values linked: Individualism? Equality of opportunity? Personal liberty?
    c. How do the above conflict?
    d. How did the Bill of Rights supplement the original Constitution?
    e. What balance is necessary between liberty and equality?
    f. What are the essential elements for a democratic election?
    g. What is meant by federalism?
    h. How is power separated?

4. Making Democratic Principles a Reality
    a. How do each of these conditions promote democracy: education? the economy? social conditions? ideology?
    b. What conditions did we overcome to survive as a democracy?

5. The Constitutional Roots of the American Experiment
    a. What incidents provoked opposition to British rule?
    b. Why were the Articles of Confederation inadequate?
    c. What prompted the Annapolis Convention?
    d. Why was Shays' Rebellion a catalyst for revision of the articles?

6. The Constitutional Convention of 1787
    a. What was the background of the convention delegates?
    b. Why are they described as "well-read, well-fed, well-bred, and well-wed"?
    c. What groups were missing from the convention?
    d. Why did the convention impose a rule of secrecy?
    e. What consensus existed among the delegates?

    f. On what issues did they compromise?

    g. Why was the Connecticut Plan adopted over those proposed by Virginia and New Jersey?

    h. How did the convention compromise the issue of slavery?

    i. What evidence exists to prove that the framers were moral philosophers? Practical men?

7.   Adopt or Not to Adopt?

    a. What restrictions on the revision of the articles had the convention violated? Why?

    b. Who were the supporters of the Federalists?

    c. Who supported the Anti-Federalists?

    d. What impact did the Federalist papers have in the debate?

    e. How did the lack of a Bill of Rights help opponents of ratification?

    f. How did the Federalists meet this objection?

    g. What factors favored the Federalists?

h. In which states was the ratification vote the closest?

PART II — PRETEST

1. One of the following words is not at the heart of American beliefs.
    a. competition
    c. liberty
    b. freedom
    d. equality

2. In the aftermath of 9/11, the public viewed politicians in what way?
    a. more favorably
    c. as being more corrupt
    b. as being unnecessary
    d. generally, with more hostility

3. Advocates of democracy argue that the public interest is best discovered by
    a. consulting top social scientists.
    b. permitting all adults to have a vote.
    c. entrusting decision making to political party leaders.
    d. the creation of philosopher-kings.

4. Democracy as a theory of government is centered on
    a. the individual.
    c. interest groups.
    b. political parties.
    d. an independent judiciary.

5. Constitutionalism as a part of democratic government serves to
    a. define and limit the government's power.
    b. expand the authority of officials.
    c. protect the rights of the majority.
    d. safeguard against revolution.

6. In Africa, the oldest democracy is
    a. Nigeria.
    c. Angola.

b. South Africa.   d. Botswana.

7. A candidate who receives 55 percent of the popular vote has obtained a
    a. majority.   c. consensus.
    b. plurality.   d. both choices a and b are correct.

8. The American Revolution began during the
    a. 1750s.   c. 1770s.
    b. 1760s.   d. 1780s.

9. The best characterization of the framers of the Constitution would be
    a. visionary idealists.   c. experienced, practical politicians.
    b. political philosophers.   d. spokesmen for the average person.

10. The Three-fifths Compromise did not deal with
    a. counting slaves.   c. representation.
    b. taxation.   d. treaty ratification.

PART III — PROGRAMMED REVIEW

Knowledge Objective: To review the many meanings of democracy and 9/11/01
  1. In a democracy, government derives its authority from its _____.
  2. Ancient Greek city-states had a _____ democracy which often turned to mob rule.
  3. Most politicians are _____ (honorable/dishonorable) men and women.
  4. The word _____ is not used in the Declaration of Independence or in the Constitution.
  5. Framers of the Constitution favored the use of _____ rather than democracy.
  6. Democracy can be viewed as a system of _____ political structures.
  7. _____ is the term used to describe government by the many.
  8. A representative democracy is commonly called a _____.
  9. A constitutional government normally _____ the power of officials.
 10. The central measure of value in a democracy is the _____.
 11. The doctrine of _____ makes the community or state the measure of value.
 12. _____ or _____ are terms used to describe the right of an individual to set his own goals.
 13. In modern America the two major values that are in a state of tension and interaction are _____ and _____.
 14. The basic democratic principle involved in elections is one person, _____ vote.
 15. In democracies, elections are decided by _____ vote.
 16. Prior to 9/11, Americans believed government to be _____ to solving problems.

Knowledge Objective: To examine conditions necessary for democracy to survive
 17. New democracies generally have a _____ (slim/good) chance of surviving.
 18. When faced with difficult times new democracies are tempted to back a strong _____ to solve their problems.

19. Democracies are most likely to survive when there are positive _____, _____, and _____ conditions.

Knowledge Objective: To explore America's Constitutional roots

20. The Founding Fathers insisted that the rights they had as English subjects be spelled out in _____ form.
21. In most American colonies _____ freedom had not been guaranteed.
22. Our Declaration of Independence asserted that the basic rights of all men included _____, _____ and _____.
23. During the period 1781-1789, Americans were governed under their first constitution, the _____.
24. Under the Articles of Confederation, a _____ was created rather than a national government.
25. The need to strengthen the machinery of government was demonstrated during the winter of 1786-1987 by a debtor's protest known as _____.

Knowledge Objective: To discover how the Constitutional Convention of 1787 went about creating a "more perfect union"

26. The framers of the Constitution were guided chiefly by _____ rather than theory.
27. At the Constitutional Convention of 1787, _____ presided; _____ was the highly respected elder statesman.
28. To encourage open discussion and compromise, proceedings of the Constitutional Convention were _____.
29. To break the deadlock over representation, the Connecticut Compromise provided that one house of Congress be based on _____; the other on _____.

Knowledge Objective: To examine the political strategy that led to adoption of the new Constitution

30. Adoption of the new Constitution required ratification by _____ states.
31. Those who opposed adoption of the Constitution were called _____.
32. Hamilton, Jay, and Madison wrote a series of essays urging adoption of the Constitution that is known collectively as _____.
33. Opposition to the new Constitution was largely concentrated in the _____ region.
34. The strategy of those who favored adoption of the Constitution was _____.
35. The Bill of Rights was demanded by the _____.

PART IV — POST-TEST

1. After 9/11, great praise was extended to New York Mayor
   a. Rudolph Guiliani.
   b. Tom Daschle.
   c. Dick Gephardt.
   d. Jim Jeffords.

2. Believers in democracy do not accept
   a. statism.
   c. individualism.

b. equality.   d. liberty.

3. In modern America, two concepts once thought to be opposites that exist in an uneasy relationship are
    a. equality and liberty.   c. oligarchy and autocracy.
    b. federal and unitary government. d. socialism and capitalism.

4. Only one of these revolutionary leaders was present at the Constitutional Convention.
    a. Thomas Jefferson   c. Patrick Henry
    b. Sam Adams   d. Alexander Hamilton

5. The incident that did most to destroy faith in government under the Articles of Confederation was
    a. the Whiskey Rebellion.   c. the Loyalist revolt.
    b. Shays' Rebellion.   d. the Indian uprising.

6. The Founding Fathers favored all but one of the following ideas.
    a. a unicameral legislature   c. an independent judiciary
    b. a strong executive   d. a more powerful Congress

7. The Connecticut Compromise found a middle ground on the issue of
    a. representation.   c. the court system.
    b. slavery.   d. the electoral college.

8. The authors of "The Federalist" include all but one of the following.
    a. Hamilton   c. Madison
    b. Jefferson   d. Jay

9. To secure ratification, supporters of the Constitution promised
    a. presidential veto power.   c. a federal income tax.
    b. a Bill of Rights.   d. a Homestead Act.

10. Only one of the following statements is true of the ratification process.
    a. The opponents tried to get a quick "no" vote.
    b. Most newspapers were Federalist opponents.
    c. Most of the opponents were in rural areas.
    d. Opposition was concentrated in the small states.

PART V — TEST ANSWERS

Pretest

1. a   6. d
2. a   7. d
3. b   8. d

4. a
5. a
6. d

9. c
10. d

Programmed Review

1. citizens
2. direct
3. honorable
4. Democracy
5. Republic
6. interdependent
7. democracy
8. republic
9. limits
10. individual
11. statism
12. Liberty; freedom
13. liberty; equality
14. one
15. majority
16. irrelevant
17. slim
18. leader
19. educational, economic, social
20. written
21. religious
22. life; liberty; pursuit of happiness
23. Articles of Confederation
24. league of friendship
25. Shays' Rebellion
26. experience
27. Washington; Franklin
28. kept secret
29. population; equality
30. nine
31. Antifederalist
32. The Federalist
33. back country
34. quick ratification
35. Antifederalist

Post-test

1. a
2. a
3. a
4. d
5. b

6. a
7. a
8. b
9. b
10. c

6

Chapter 2
The Living Constitution

PART I — GUIDEPOSTS

1. Checking Power With Power
    a. The Constitution is both a symbol and an instrument. How does it function at each level?
    b. Explain with examples the manner in which separation of powers and checks and balances were combined by the Constitution makers? Why did they adopt this device?
    c. What modifications resulted from the rise of political parties; the shift in presidential election arrangements; the appearance of administrative agencies: the increased importance of the presidential office? What factors have contributed to the emergence of presidential power?

2. Judicial Review and the "Guardians of the Constitution"
    a. What is it? What are the origins of judicial review?
    b. How does it differ from British precedent?
    c. Who originally supported it? Who opposed it?
    d. What role was played by John Marshall in *Marbury v. Madison?* Why is it a landmark decision?
    e. Why does Thurgood Marshall reject the view that the meaning of the Constitution was fixed at the Philadelphia Convention?
    f. What is the role of judicial review in the European Union? When will the the European Union have a constitution?

3. Checks and Balances
    a. Why was inefficiency built into our political system?
    b. What modifications of the original American system resulted from the rise of national political parties; the shift in presidential election arrangements; the appearance of administrative agencies; the increased importance of the presidential office?
    c. Contrast the British and American systems of government in the following respects:
        (1) British Prime Minister/American President
        (2) British Cabinet/American Cabinet
        (3) British Courts/U.S. Supreme Court
        (4) House of Lords/Senate
        (5) House of Commons/House of Representatives

4. The Constitution as an Instrument of Government
    a. In what four ways has our original written Constitution been modified informally? Give examples of each change.
    b. In what sense can it be argued that the Constitution has changed only slightly?

7

c. Why has our Constitution managed to survive with relatively few amendments since 1787? Also, what is meant by "original intent" doctrine?

5. Changing The Letter of the Constitution
   a. What are two methods of proposing amendments? Why has one never been used?
   b. How are amendments ratified? Which is the more common method?
   c. What changes in national power have been made by amendments of the Constitution? Also, how long are most ratification processes?
   d. How has state power been limited?
   e. How has the power of the voters been altered?
   f. Why did the Twenty-Seventh Amendment take 203 years to be ratified?
   g. Who was Gregory Watson?

6. Ratification Politics
   a. ERA, why did it fail adoption?

PART II — PRETEST

1. The branch of government most likely to have dominated the framers' opinion was the
   a. bureaucracy.
   b. executive.
   c. judicial.
   d. legislative.

2. How many states did the ERA lack regarding final ratification?
   a. seven
   b. four
   c. one
   d. three

3. Law that is higher than human law is dubbed _____ law.
   a. statutory
   b. universal
   c. natural
   d. constitutional

4. With one exception, ratification of constitutional amendments has been by action of
   a. the president.
   b. the Supreme Court.
   c. state conventions.
   d. state legislatures.

Match the items in the left column with the correct items from the right column.

   5. separation of powers
   6. checks and balances
   7. shared powers
   8. *Marbury v. Madison*
   9. impeachment
   10. informal Constitution

   a. based on custom
   b. lame duck Congress
   c. allocates power among branches
   d. independent branches that are interdependent
   e. established judicial review
   f. charges brought by House
   g. president signs congressional bill

PART III — PROGRAMMED REVIEW

Knowledge Objective: To analyze the original constitutional arrangements that diffused political power

1. In the United States, the symbol of national loyalty and unity has been the _____.

2. The constitutional arrangement that delegated certain powers to the national government and reserved the rest for the states is called _____.

3. The framers of the Constitution did not fully trust either _____ or the _____.

4. The allocation of constitutional authority among three branches of the national government is known as _____ _____ _____.

5. The framers devised a system of shared power that is described by the term _____ _____ _____.

6. The varying terms of office for national officials were intended to prevent rapid changes by a popular _____.

7. In the United States the ultimate keeper of our constitutional conscience is the _____ _____ .

8. The court case that established the practice of judicial review was _____ *v.* _____.

Knowledge Objective: To examine the developments that have modified the original checks and balances system

9. The president, Congress, and even judges have been drawn together in the American system by _____ _____.

10. Originally neither the _____ nor _____ were elected directly by the people.

11. Legislative, executive, and judicial functions are combined in some agencies, weakening the concept of _____ _____ _____.

12. In the modern United States, the branch of government that has acquired the greatest power is the _____.

13. The British system concentrates power and control in the _____ _____.

Knowledge Objective: To trace evolution of the Constitution by custom and interpretation

14. The customs, traditions, and rules that have evolved over the past two centuries are referred to as a(an) _____ Constitution.

15. The structure of the national judicial system was defined by action of _____.

16. The most discussed example of congressional elaboration of the Constitution during the Nixon years was the _____ process.

17. _____ realities have increased the importance of the presidency.

18. The Constitution has been adapted to changing times largely through judicial _____.

Knowledge Objective: To analyze the amendment process and the constitutional changes made by it

19. Initiating a constitutional amendment requires a _____ vote by both houses of Congress.
20. Although it has never been used, an amendment can be proposed by a _____ _____ fraction.
21. A proposed amendment must be ratified in three-fourths of the states by either their _____ or _____ _____.
22. Congress (has, has not) _____ proposed a great number of amendments.

Knowledge Objective: To examine politics of the amendment process in cases of ERA and the D.C. Amendments
23. In the case of _____ Congress altered the normal process by extending the time for ratification.
24. Equal Rights Amendment ratification has been blocked chiefly by a group of _____ states.

PART IV — POST-TEST

1. The framers of the Constitution depended heavily on which of the following assumptions about human behavior?
    a. Ambition will serve to check ambition.
    b. Most people want to do the right thing.
    c. People are normally apathetic.
    d. Human savagery always lurks below the thin veneer of civilization.

2. The Founding Fathers created a system that
    a. encouraged participatory democracy.
    b. favored the popular majority.
    c. restricted decision making by popular majority.
    d. emphasized prompt, decisive government action.

3. The British democratic system differs from the American system in that
    a. the queen reigns but doesn't rule.
    b. Parliament has only one house.
    c. government authority is concentrated in Parliament.
    d. the High Court exercises judicial review.

4. The original checks and balances system has been modified by all but one of the following:
    a. the rise of political parties
    b. creation of regulatory agencies
    c. direct election of senators
    d. giving representatives a four-year term

5. As originally drafted, the Constitution was expected to
    a. cover all foreseeable situations.
    b. be a legal code, combining the framework of government and specific laws.

c. be a general framework of government.

d. be a philosophical statement of the relationships among individuals,

6. The Constitution of the United States has been altered without formal amendment by all but one of the following methods:

    a. congressional elaboration

    b. presidential practice

    c. custom and usage

    d. interposition by states

7. Compared to many state constitutions, the national constitution is more

    a. recent.

    b. complicated.

    c. specific.

    d. flexible.

8. The major tool of the courts in checking the power of other government branches has been

    a. impeachment.

    b. habeas corpus.

    c. judicial review.

    d. common law.

9. The constitutional arrangement that limits the power of American officials is known as

    a. separation of powers.

    b. prohibitions on authority.

    c. sharing of powers.

    d. implied powers.

10. During the Revolutionary period, legislatures

    a. were curbed by the checks and balances system.

    b. became the dominant branch of government.

    c. suffered from a steady decrease in power.

    d. governed firmly and wisely.

PART V — TEST ANSWERS

Pretest

1.	d	6.	d
2.	c	7.	g
3.	c	8.	e
4.	d	9.	f
5.	c	10.	a

Programmed Review

1.	Constitution	13.	legislative branch
2.	federalism	14.	informal
3.	public officials; majority	15.	Congress
4.	separation of powers	16.	impeachment
5.	checks and balances	17.	Global
6.	majority	18.	interpretation

7. Supreme Court
8. *Marbury v. Madison*
9. political parties
10. president; senators
11. checks and balances
12. executive

19. two-thirds
20. constitutional convention
21. legislatures,ratifying conventions
22. has not
23. ERA
24. southern

Post-test

1. a
2. c
3. c
4. d
5. c

6. d
7. d
8. c
9. a
10. b

Chapter 3
American Federalism

PART I — GUIDEPOSTS

1. Introduction/Why Federalism?
   a. Distinguish between a federal government and a confederation and give an example of each. Also, what is the meaning of the "devolution revolution"?
   b. Why was federalism rather than a unitary state the only realistic arrangement in 1787?
   c. What advantages has federalism offered with respect to:
      (1) American expansion
      (2) diversity
      (3) social-economic experiments
      (4) political leadership
   d. How have federalism issues affected Russia, Canada, and the U.K.?
   e. What was the importance of the Educational Flexibility Partnership Demonstration Act of 1999?
   f. Why did the power of the federal government expand after 9/11?

2. Defining Federalism/Constitutional Structure of Federalism
   a. What is meant by expressed national powers? Implied powers? Inherent powers? Also, review unitary and confederation forms.
   b. How have each of the following powers contributed to expansion of the national government?
      (1) war
      (2) commerce
      (3) taxation — general welfare
   c. What powers are left to the state?
   d. What constitutional restraints were put on the national government? The state government?
   e. Review the various kinds of federalism. Give an example of full faith and credit; interstate privileges and immunities; national supremacy and extradition clauses.
   f. What are the advantages of federalism?

3. The Role of the Federal Courts
   a. What issues were at stake in *McCulloch v. Maryland?* How were they decided?
   b. Over the years when has the Supreme Court favored a position that makes it, rather than Congress, the ultimate umpire in contests between the states and the national government?
   c. When does preemption occur?

4.   The Politics of Federalism
     a. How have each of the following factors expanded government
             (1) urbanization and population growth
             (2) world power status
             (3) transportation — communication changes
             (4) concentration of private economic power
     b. What was the original nationalist (centralist) position on federalism?
     c. What was the states' rights (decentralists') position?
     d. What is the devolution revolution?
     e. What are the key arguments of the centralists and decentralists?
     f. How is the growth of government related to the pattern of U.S. federalism?

5.   Federal Grants and Regulations
     a. What is the distinction between categorical formula grants, project grants, and block grants?
     b. Why are grants important to the states?
     c. What groups favor the various types of grants?
     d. How have federal mandates affected the grant process?
     e. What has been the significance of welfare reform within the federal system?
     f. What is the importance of the Unfunded Mandates Reform Act?

6.   The Future of Federalism
     a. Why is the politics of federalism more complicated for minorities today?
     b. Why are some business interests asking for federal regulations?
     c. What new responsibilities are the states facing?
     d. Why do Americans have strong attachments to the federal system?

PART II — PRETEST

1. The best argument for retention of our federal system would be that it
    a. prevents the centralization of power.
    b. provides cheap, efficient government.
    c. simplifies political party organization.
    d. provides both unity and diversity.

2. The national government has *all but one* of the following powers.
    a. implied   c. reserved
    b. inherent   d. delegated

3. The state governments have *only one* of the following sets of powers.
    a. delegated and reserved   c. direct and inherent
    b. reserved and concurrent   d. expressed and implied

4. The states' rights interpretation of the Constitution conflicts with one of these concepts.

14

a. broad construction   c. treaty among sovereign states
b. reserved powers   d. state governments closer to people

5. The power of the national government that has not been a chief source of its expansion is
    a. to coin money.   c. to regulate interstate commerce.
    b. to declare war.   d. to levy taxes.

6. Centralists believe which of the following best defines the power of the national government?
    a. all power specifically delegated by the Constitution
    b. delegated powers plus powers implied from the delegated ones
    c. whatever needs to be done to promote the general welfare
    d. dependent on which party is in power

7. In our history, northerners, southerners, business people, and workers have
    a. consistently agreed on the role of the state governments.
    b. held to a single opinion with respect to national powers.
    c. changed sides in the debate over national-state powers.
    d. shown no discernible pattern of opinion at all.

8. Any group that "has the votes" in Washington is almost certain to favor
    a. a strong national government.
    b. states' rights.
    c. a Supreme Court critical of congressional power.
    d. local government as being closer to the people.

9. The great expansion of our grant-in-aid system occurred during
    a. the New Deal.   c. World War I.
    b. the 1960s.   d. World War II.

10. A federal grant that gives a state the right to spend money within a broad category is called a
    a. project grant.   c. community action grant.
    b. block grant.   d. grant-in-aid.

PART III — PROGRAMMED REVIEW

Knowledge Objective: To contrast federalism with alternate forms of government and to discover what advantages it offers Americans
    1. A _____ government divides power between a central government and constituent governments.
    2. The central government of a confederation exercises no power over _____.
    3. A _____ government vests all power in the central government.

4. The relationship between American state and city governments is an example of the _____ form of government.

5. A federal government provides for _____ without uniformity.

6. Under our federal system such questions as divorce, gun control, and school dress codes are _____ issues.

7. The American people are most concerned with _____ politics.

Knowledge Objective: To define how the Constitution allots power and the limitations it imposes

8. The three major powers of Congress upon which national expansion is based are _____, _____, and _____.

9. The Constitution delegates to Congress both _____ powers and _____ powers.

10. As an independent nation, the national government has certain _____ powers.

11. The powers shared by the national and state governments are called _____ powers.

12. The Constitution requires that the national government guarantee to every state a _____ form of government.

13. The _____ clause requires states to enforce civil judgments of other states.

14. The process by which a criminal is surrendered by one state to another is called _____.

15. A binding agreement among states that is approved by Congress is known as a(n) _____.

Knowledge Objective: To trace and explain the growth of the national government and the expanding role of the federal courts

16. Sending federal functions back to the states and local government is called the _____ revolution.

17. The _____ interpretation of the Constitution argued that the national government was created by the states.

18. The centralists' interpretation of the Constitution argued that the national government was an agent of the _____ rather than the states.

19. The concept of implied powers for the national government was first established by the Supreme Court in _____.

20. The Chief Justice of the Supreme Court who first set forth the doctrine of national supremacy was _____.

21. The umpire of the Federal system that has favored the national government is the _____.

22. The expansion of the national government can be explained in large part by our evolution from an agrarian society to a(n) _____ society.

23. Our urban society has created a demand for programs operated by the _____ government.

24. Today many Americans identify closely with the national government because of their daily exposure to _____.

25. In 1996, fear of the expansion of the _____ _____moderated the expansion of government spending.
26. The court action giving Congress the right to assume total power over a state issue is called _____.

Knowledge Objective: To differentiate among the various types of federal grant programs and controls

27. _____ _____ grants involve matching federal-state funds for a specific program.
28. Local communities can receive federal funds directly outside any formula distribution under _____ grants.
29. Federal funds distributed according to formula for a broad purpose are called _____ grants.
30. AFDC was ended under the presidency of _____.
31. Federal regulations that bar state-local discrimination in employment are an example of _____ _____.
32. The national government has indirectly regulated automobile speed limits and minimum drinking ages through its financing of _____ construction.
33. Under the Reagan administration, national control of state and local governments (was, was not) _____ diminished significantly.

Knowledge Objective: To consider the relationship that has developed between national and urban government

34. During the 1960s federal grant policy created a financial bond between the national government and _____.
35. In recent years city officials have found state governments to be (more, less) _____ responsive to their problems.
36. Ronald Reagan "presided over a huge growth of big government at the _____levels."
37. Most Americans have _____ (strong, weak) attachments to the federal system.
38. In recent years the quality of state government has (improved, deteriorated)_____.

PART IV — POST-TEST

1. The decentralist basic premise is that the Constitution is a
   a. statement of principles.
   b. union of people.
   c. treaty among sovereign states.
   d. document inspired by God.

2. The basic centralist premise is that the Constitution is a supreme law established by the
   a. people.
   b. state.
   c. Creator.
   d. Continental Congress.

3. Federalism can be defended in *all but one* of the following ways.

a. Political experimentation is encouraged.
b. Governed and governors are in closer contact.
c. Allowances are made for differences.
d. A national majority can more easily implement its program.

4. The supreme law of the land is composed of *all but one* of the following.
   a. the Supreme Court
   b. the U.S. Constitution
   c. U.S. law
   d. U.S. treaties

5. John Marshall's decision in *McCulloch v. Maryland* was that
   a. the government did not have authority to operate a bank.
   b. state tax powers are unlimited within their boundaries.
   c. Scottish naturalized immigrants can sit on the Supreme Court.
   d. the national government has the authority to carry out its powers in a variety of ways.

6. In interstate relations each state must accept without question one of the following.
   a. demand for extradition
   b. enforcement of civil judgment
   c. a Nevada divorce
   d. immediate voting rights for the other state's citizens

7. The average citizen of the United States today
   a. follows closely the activities of the state legislature.
   b. regards the citizens of other states as foreigners.
   c. is in close contact with local and state officials.
   d. is best informed about the national political scene.

8. Throughout our history, business had advocated
   a. states' rights.
   b. national supremacy.
   c. neither.
   d. both.

9. The present mood of the country with respect to federalism is best described as
   a. confused.
   b. pro city hall.
   c. less revenue-sharing.
   d. states' rights.

10. Under its partial preemption regulations the national government has sought to control
    a. surface mining.
    b. air quality standards.
    c. highway speed limits.
    d. occupational safety.

PART V — TEST ANSWERS

Pretest

1. d
2. c
3. b
4. a
5. a

6. c
7. c
8. a
9. b
10. b

Programmed Review

1. federal
2. individuals
3. unitary
4. unitary
5. unity
6. state
7. national
8. war, commerce, tax
9. express; implied
10. inherent
11. concurrent
12. republican
13. full faith and credit
14. extradition
15. interstate compact
16. devolution
17. decentralists
18. people
19. *McCulloch v. Maryland*

20. John Marshall
21. Supreme Court
22. industrial
23. national
24. television
25. national debt
26. preemption
27. Categorical formula
28. project
29. block
30. Clinton
31. direct orders
32. highway
33. was not
34. cities
35. more
36. State
37. strong
38. improved

Post-test

1. c
2. a
3. d
4. a
5. d

6. b
7. d
8. d
9. a
10. b

Chapter 4
Political Culture and Ideology

PART I – GUIDEPOSTS

1. Introduction/American Beliefs and Behavior Patterns
   a. What attitudes do Americans share?
   b. What basic beliefs/values do they hold in common?
   c. What kinds of conflict exist within our ideology and culture?
   d. As compared with other Western democracies, in which political virtues do we seem to excel?
   e. What is significant about Putnam's concept of "social capital"? How did the events of 9/11 relate to the concept?

2. The American Political Culture
   a. What is meant by political culture?
   b. What is the "democratic consensus"?
   c. From where do individuals learn the political culture?
   d. What new rights did FDR sponsor for Americans?

3. What is the American Dream (see Oprah Winfrey insert)?
   a. How do the central values of political equality and a free market system conflict?
   b. Why should the American system be described as mixed?
   c. What do Americans believe about rewarding people of ability? Private property? Inheritance?
   d. What trend seems to be developing in the way American wealth is distributed between the wealthy and the poor?
   e. What tensions does this create in a society that believes in political equality? How did the Enron scandal demonstrate inequality?

4. Political Ideology and Attitudes Toward Government
   a. In trying to define liberal and conservative attitudes, what tests apply?
   b. Why are clear-cut labels hard to define?
   c. How are today's liberals different than earlier ones? Contrast their modern attitudes regarding the role of government.
   d. What attitudes do liberals have toward the possibility of progress?
   e. Explain the fundamental assumptions of libertarianism, environmentalism, socialism, and conservatism.

5. Ideology, The American People, and Tolerance
   a. What clear-cut differences separate conservatives and liberals on the issue of tolerance?
   b. How do they differ on civil rights and liberties?
   c. Why is policy-making characterized by coalitions rather than fixed alignments?
   d. Why are there so few extreme conservatives and liberals?
   e. Why did the two parties target centrist/moderate voters in the 2000/2002 elections?

PART II — PRETEST

1. Most Americans share *all but one* of these following values.
   - a. religion
   - b. free enterprise
   - c. Big Business
   - d. free press

2. Americans for the most part *do not believe* in
   - a. pragmatism.
   - b. free speech.
   - c. active political participation.
   - d. passive government.

3. Americans do believe in
   - a. self help.
   - b. government regulation.
   - c. socialism.
   - d. a class system.

4. Americans believe that this condition is necessary to make the system work.
   - a. unemployment
   - b. discrimination
   - c. education
   - d. uniformity of belief

5. According to most Americans we are not a land of
   - a. cooperative endeavors.
   - b. opportunity.
   - c. common sense.
   - d. rugged individualism.

6. For the most part Americans are
   - a. anti-intellectual.
   - b. theorists.
   - c. selfish.
   - d. careful spenders.

7. Political culture refers to shared
   - a. beliefs.
   - b. values.
   - c. norms.
   - d. all of the above

8. The American dream consists of
   - a. enthusiasm for capitalism.
   - b. competitive markets.
   - c. limited government involvement.
   - d. all of these.

9. Grover Norquist would best represent the ideology of
   - a. liberalism.
   - b. socialism.
   - c. conservatism.
   - d. libertarianism.

10. The New Right represents a group with a(n) _____ base.
    - a. rural
    - b. economic
    - c. mystical
    - d. religious

PART III — PROGRAMMED REVIEW

Knowledge Objective: What are the basic features of American culture and ideology?
1. Classical liberalism stresses the importance of the _____.
2. Liberal political philosophers claimed individuals have certain _____ _____ and the state must be limited.

21

3. The Constitution, like the American Revolution, defines our nation and its _____.
4. The idea that every individual has a right to equal protection and voting power is called _____ _____.
5. Americans are optimistic about _____, but not about our government.
6. Widely shared beliefs and values are called our political _____.
7. Perhaps our most commonly held belief is that of _____.
8. In the American system of values, the role of government is to _____ _____ _____.
9. Americans believe that (more, less) _____ direct political power should be in the hands of the people.
10. In a broad sense America (does, does not) _____ have an official philosophy.

Knowledge Objective: To trace the demand for additional rights in American experience: the American Dream
11. One of the first rights to be won in America was the right to _____.
12. Inequality of _____ was the result of the growth of corporations.
13. The unregulated growth of American capitalism was challenged by the _____.
14. Huge _____ do not fit into our basic democratic theory.
15. Franklin Roosevelt declared that all Americans had the right to adequate _____ care.
16. Roosevelt also said that every American had the right to a useful _____.
17. The gap between rich and poor in the United States has _____ in recent years.
18. Americans dream of acquiring _____.
19. The American Dream includes (inequality, equality) _____ of income.
20. Most Americans today support a semiregulated or _____ free enterprise system.

Knowledge Objective: To distinguish between liberal and conservative public policies
21. Modern _____ political leaders favor greater government activity.
22. _____ leaders believe that national progress is possible.
23. Environmentalism is exemplified by _____ parties in Europe and America.
24. Private property rights and free enterprise are basic beliefs of _____.
25. _____ believe that most people who fail are personally responsible for their failure.
26. A brand of conservatism that is more radical, the New _____ has emerged in recent years.
27. Conservatives are criticized for not endorsing policies against racism and _____.
28. _____ favor an expanded government that would own the means of production and distribution.
29. _____ favor a severely curbed role for government in domestic and foreign affairs.

Knowledge Objective: To define the basic political tension in modern America
30. Our national political life is based on a (carefully defined, vague) _____ theory.
31. American political parties are (more, less) _____ ideological than European parties.
32. Tolerance is most prevalent among _____ (liberals/conservatives).
33. Conservatives show more concern for the rights of _____ _____ _____ while liberals show more concern for the rights of the _____.
34. Conservatives prize the private sector over the _____ sector.

35. Conservatives believe that America has become too _____.

PART IV — POST-TEST

1. Which one of the following groups wants the least government?
   - a. Libertarians
   - b. Conservatives
   - c. Liberals
   - d. Socialists

2. Which group demands the most government?
   - a. Socialists
   - b. Conservatives
   - c. Libertarians
   - d. Greens

3. Former senator Rudman questions the GOP alliance with which group?
   - a. New Right
   - b. Environmentalists
   - c. Conservatives
   - d. Libertarians

4. A major barrier to equality of opportunity today is
   - a. failure to vote.
   - b. lack of education.
   - c. unequal start.
   - d. high taxes.

5. When the Great Depression began we had
   - a. unemployment compensation.
   - b. bank deposit guarantees.
   - c. regulation of security exchanges.
   - d. the vote for women.

6. The American president most responsible for greatly expanding the rights of all Americans was
   - a. Truman.
   - b. Eisenhower.
   - c. Hoover.
   - d. FDR.

7. Those who favor expansion of government control over drinking, drugs, abortion, prayer, and life style are
   - a. Conservatives.
   - b. New Right.
   - c. Liberals.
   - d. Libertarians.

8. The most important source of the American political culture is the
   - a. school.
   - b. family.
   - c. mass media.
   - d. church or synagogue.

9. The political group who today advocates the withdrawal of our forces from Europe and the decriminalization of drug possession is
   - a. Conservatives.
   - b. Liberals.
   - c. Libertarians.
   - d. Socialists.

10. In today's world the greatest conflict is between the free market enterprise system and
    - a. socialism.
    - b. equality of opportunity.
    - c. private property.
    - d. voting rights.

PART V — TEST ANSWERS

Pretest

1. c
2. d
3. a
4. c
5. a

6. a
7. d
8. d
9. c
10. d

Programmed Review

1. individual
2. natural rights
3. values
4. political equality
5. people
6. culture
7. liberty
8. serve the people
9. more
10. does not
11. vote
12. wealth
13. Great Depression
14. corporations
15. medical
16. job
17. grown
18. property

19. inequality
20. mixed
21. liberal
22. Liberal
23. Green
24. conservatives
25. Conservatives
26. Right
27. sexism
28. Socialists
29. Libertarians
30. vague
31. less
32. liberals
33. victims of crime; accused
34. public
35. permissive

Post-test

1. a
2. a
3. a
4. c
5. d

6. d
7. b
8. b
9. c
10. b

Chapter 5
The American Political Landscape

PART I — GUIDEPOSTS

1. Introduction/A Land of Diversity
    a. How has immigration made us so diverse?
    b. How does diversity promote tension?
    c. What was the significance of Proposition 187?
    d. What is political socialization; reinforcing/cross-cutting cleavages?

2. Where Are We From/Where We Live
    a. How does geography explain our diversity?
    b. Why is the South the most distinct district in the United States?
    c. How have the South's voting patterns changed in recent years?
    d. What makes California distinctive?
    e. What has "white flight" done to the modern day city?
    f. How has the growth of metropolitan areas rearranged black-white relationships?
    g. How did 9/11 prove the U.S. was vulnerable?
    h. What problems do cities have today?

3. Who We Are; Race and Ethnicity
    a. Who are the major racial groups in the United States?
    b. What percentage of the population does each group compose?
    c. Trace black migration patterns within the United States.
    d. What are the major areas of disagreement between blacks and whites?
    e. How have the blacks increased their political power? Which party do most blacks favor and why?
    f. Why have Asian Americans been the most successful racial group economically and educationally?
    g. Why are Hispanics "underrepresented"?

4. Gender/Sexual Orientation
    a. How has the political power of women changed in the last two decades?
    b. Why is income a major issue on the women's political agenda?
    c. What policy issues divide men and women? Is there a gender gap?
    d. What is the current status of gay and lesbian rights in America?
    e. How has the traditional family structure changed?

5. Other Institutional Differences
    a. What was the impact of Senator Joe Lieberman's 2000 vice presidential candidacy?
    b. What role does religion play in the United States?
    c. What shifts in wealth and income have occurred since 1980?
    d. How does the distribution of income affect the stability of a democratic nation?

e. Why is poverty a political issue?
f. What distinctions exist between an industrial society and a post-industrial society?
g. What are the occupational patterns of women and racial minorities?
h. Why has social class been relatively unimportant in the United States?
i. Why have the elderly been such a political success?
j. How important is education to a diverse society?

6. Unity in a Land of Diversity
   a. What factors unify our diverse population?
   b. How does the melting pot theory differ from the salad bowl theory? Which best describes the United States?

PART II — PRETEST

1. The tendency of every person to make sweeping judgments based on their limited personal experience is called
   a. ethnocentricism.
   b. wisdom.
   c. experience.
   d. selfishness.

2. The most distinct geographical region in the United States is the
   a. Midwest.
   b. Southwest.
   c. South.
   d. West.

3. Only one of these cities *does not* have a majority black population?
   a. Phoenix
   b. Baltimore
   c. Richmond
   d. New Orleans

4. Which of the following is not a gender issue?
   a. sexual harassment
   b. child support
   c. peace
   d. English as the official language

5. The most politically underrepresented group has been
   a. Asians.
   c. Hispanics.
   b. blacks.
   d. women.

6. The most potent politically active group has been
   a. college students.
   b. the elderly.
   c. the poor.
   d. the common man.

7. A popular theory that explains the unity achieved by Americans is the
   a. salad bowl.
   b. melting pot.
   c. welding.
   d. ethnicity.

8. Compared to most industrialized countries the United States does not have a high degree of
   _____ awareness
   a. social class
   b. religious intolerance

c. personal achievement   d. acceptance of a leisure class

9. In recent years the South has given its vote for president to
    a. Republicans.   c. no decisive pattern.
    b. Democrats.   d. varied.

10. Black migration from the South occurred chiefly after
    a. 1865.   c. 1970.
    b. 1950.   d. 1900.

PART III — PROGRAMMED REVIEW

Knowledge Objective: To trace the roots of the American people
1. Proposition 187 in California dealt with the issue of _____.
2. The tendency to generalize from our own experience is called _____.
3. The belief that we have a foreordained role to become a world power is called _____.
4. The most distinct section of the United States is the _____.
5. After the Civil War the South normally supported the _____ party.
6. The West has developed a strong sense of _____.
7. Most Americans now live in _____ areas.
8. The migration of white Americans to the suburbs after World War II is known as the _____ _____.
9. Migration of the whites from the cities has resulted in a(n) _____ tax base.

Knowledge Objective: To distinguish the various elements in our diverse society
10. Children normally learn their political values within the _____.
11. When cultural values are in conflict the result is called _____ _____ cleavages.
12. Politically, the United States compared to Ireland has less emphasis on _____.
13. The first Jewish vice presidential candidate for a major party was Senator _____ in 2000.
14. The mass migration of blacks to the city gave them greater _____ power but left them with limited _____ power.
15. Nearly _____ of the blacks fall below the poverty level.
16. According to the text, Hispanics are politically _____.
17. Hispanics can be of any _____.
18. Generally speaking older ethnic groups have greater _____ power than newer ethnic groups.
19. Compared to the women in other countries, American women vote _____ (more, less).
20. The largest segment of Americans are _____.
21. Women for the most part (do, do not) _____ support female candidates.
22. As women age, the earnings gap _____.
23. Significant political difference between men and women is called the _____.
24. A defining characteristic of religion in America is the variety of _____.
25. African-Americans traditionally support the _____ Party.

27

Knowledge Objective: To investigate social and economic differences

26. Widespread income distribution results in political _____.
27. One of the most important means for Americans to achieve economic and social mobility is _____.
28. Originally most Americans worked as _____.
29. Today America is known as a _____ society.
30. In terms of social class most Americans believe that they are _____ class.
31. In recent years the American Dream has been challenged by foreign _____.

PART IV — POST-TEST

1. Democratic strengths in the South have been greatest in elections for
   a. president.
   b. U.S. Senate.
   c. representative.
   d. no pattern.

2. The state with the largest population is
   a. New York.
   b. Pennsylvania.
   c. California.
   d. Texas.

3. Fundamentalist Christians have an agenda that includes *all but one* of the following.
   a. return of school prayer
   b. outlaw abortion
   c. outlaw guns
   d. restrict homosexuals

4. The population of American cities has *all but one* of the following characteristics.
   a. poor
   b. black
   c. independent
   d. democratic

5. Black unemployment is a result of *all but one* of the following.
   a. limited education
   b. youth
   c. depressed urban areas
   d. limited political power

6. Most Asian Americans live in *all but one* of the following states.
   a. Michigan
   b. Hawaii
   c. Washington
   d. California

7. Recent Asian-American migration has been from *all but one* of the following.
   a. Korea
   b. Japan
   c. Asia
   d. Southeast

8. The fastest growing ethnic group in the United States is
   a. Hispanics.
   b. African Americans.
   c. Asian
   d. Native Americans.

9. The gray lobby has *all but one* of these political assets.

   a. mostly male
   b. disposable income
   c. discretionary time
   d. focused issues

10. American unity is strengthened by *all but one* of the following.
    a. the American Dream
    b. work ethic
    c. economic opportunity
    d. foreign investment

PART V — TEST ANSWERS

Pretest

1. a	6. b
2. c	7. b
3. a	8. a
4. d	9. a
4. b	10. b

Programmed Review

1. immigration	17. race
2. Ethnocentricism	18. economic
3. manifest destiny	19. less
4. South	20. women
5. Democratic	21. do not
6. Individualism	22. widens
7. Metropolitan	23. gender gap
8. white flight	24. denominations
9. declining	25. Democratic
10. family	26. stability
11. cross-cutting	27. education
12. religion	28. farmers
13. Lieberman	29. post-industrial
14. political; economic	30. middle
15. one third	31. competition
16. underrepresented	

Post-test

1. c	6. a
2. c	7. b
3. c	8. a
4. c	9. a
5. d	10. d

Chapter 6
Interest Groups: The Politics of Influence

PART I — GUIDEPOSTS

1. The "Mischiefs of Faction"
    a. Madison foresaw "factions" as an inevitable development
    b. What is an interest group?
    c. Why are they organized?
    d. What makes public interest groups distinctive?
    e. How do social movements differ from interest groups?

2. Types of Interest Groups
    a. What are the important economic interest groups?
    b. What are the major professional/ideological interest groups?
    c. Name three non-occupational/public interest groups.
    d. What groups are organized to influence foreign policy?
    e. Why do single cause interest groups offer a challenge to democracy?
    f. Name government/government employee interest groups.

3. Characteristics and Power of Interest Groups
    a. What advantages do large interest groups have? What weaknesses?
    b. How is overlapping membership a limiting factor?
    c. What factors contribute to an effective interest group?
    d. How do interest groups attract members and get financial support?
    e. How do interest groups use each of the following techniques in lobbying: persuasion; elections; litigation; mass/e-mailing; rule making?
    f. What is cooperative lobbying?
    g. Why are militia groups a cause for concern?

4. The Influence of Lobbyists
    a. How does modern lobbying differ from that of the 1800s?
    b. What are the rules for successful lobbying?
    c. What skills does a lobbyist need?

5. Money and Politics/2002 Campaign Finance Reform Legislation
    a. What is a PAC? How do PACs allocate their contributions?
    b. Why is PAC money important in elections/legislation?
    c. What was the impact of 2002 on soft money/issue advocacy ads/PACs?
    d. How did the 2002 law affect interest groups/individual contributions?

6. Curing the "Mischiefs of Faction"--Two Centuries Later
    a. How would Madison react to the modern lobbying scene?
    b. What constitutional issue is raised when we try to control interest groups?
    c. Why is it difficult for Congress to reform campaign finance?
    d. What was the Lobbying Disclosure Act of 1995?

PART II — PRETEST

1. The loyalty of interest group members is often diminished by their
   - a. overlapping allegiances.
   - b. inability to pay dues.
   - c. limited time.
   - d. religious convictions.

2. Nearly all adult Americans belong to a/an _____ interest group.
   - a. social
   - b. religious
   - c. ideological
   - d. occupational

3. In recent years the great expansion of PACs has been in the _____ sector.
   - a. labor
   - b. professional
   - c. business
   - d. farming

4. The chief influence of PACs in election campaigns has been their
   - a. contributions.
   - b. advice.
   - c. door-bell ringing.
   - d. professional aid.

5. In its efforts to control factions and interest groups, the United States has rejected
   - a. their prohibition.
   - b. publicizing their activity.
   - c. regulating their activity.
   - d. lobbying.

6. AIPAC is an interest group that promotes the interest of
   - a. the Arab states.
   - b. Israel.
   - c. senior citizens.
   - d. labor unions.

7. Which one of the following interest groups cuts across religious, ethnic, and economic groups?
   - a. American Medical Association
   - b. American Soybean Association
   - c. Knights of Columbus
   - d. Young Americans for Freedom

8. The interest group that has advocated an open political process and electoral reform is
   - a. the National Rifle Association.
   - b. Nuclear Freeze.
   - c. the Trilateral Commission.
   - d. Common Cause.

9. Efforts to represent the general welfare are thwarted by _____ groups.
   - a. public interest
   - b. single cause
   - c. occupational
   - d. organized

10. The 2002 campaign finance reform law bans
    - a. hard money.
    - b. soft money.
    - c. PACs.
    - d. all issue ads.

PART III — PROGRAMMED REVIEW

Knowledge Objective: To examine factions as a force in politics
1. James Madison's famous essay on the role of factions is called _____ _____ _____.
2. Madison believed that popular government normally resulted in instability, injustice, and confusion because it encouraged the growth of _____.

31

3. Any group whose members share attitudes and try to achieve certain aims and objectives is called an _____ group.
4. Movements normally arise when segments of the population find that the dominant political culture does not share their _____.
5. Movement politics normally are successful in raising the political _____ of their followers.
6. The "paycheck protection" initiative was against _____ _____.
7. Interest groups are also called _____ _____.

Knowledge Objective: To describe the various kinds of interest groups
8. Nearly every employed person belongs to an _____ interest group.
9. The major farm interest group is _____ _____ _____; labor's largest group is _____; and the largest business group is _____ _____ _____ _____.
10. Common Cause is an example of a _____ _____ group.
11. The highly articulate spokesman for a conglomerate of consumer interest groups and the Green Party's presidential candidate in 2000 was _____.
12. The ACLU is an example of an _____ interest group.
13. _____ _____ groups focus on highly specialized political issues.

Knowledge Objective: To investigate the techniques of interest group politics
14. Central tests of a group's power are its _____ and _____.
15. The cohesiveness of any interest group is weakened by _____ memberships.
16. The AARP uses _____ to combat the free-rider problem.
17. Civil liberties, environmental, and black groups have used _____ as a weapon to achieve their goals.
18. The Federal _____ lists regulations of executive departments/agencies.
19. The employee of an interest group who presents its point of view to legislators is called a _____.
20. The employment cycle from government to interest group is known as the _____ _____.
21. Lobbyists have the _____ _____ needed by legislators for policy making.

Knowledge Objective: To examine the scope of PACs
22. The newest form of interest groups that back candidates and raise money are _____.
23. The great expansion of PACs during the 1980s was among _____ interest groups.
24. Contributors to PACs normally (do, do not) _____ demand immediate payoffs if their candidate wins.
25. Big labor's political arm is called _____.
26. PACs can _____ their contributions in order to boost their clout with elected officials.
27. _____ is not a major criterion used by big corporations in financing the campaigns of Congressional candidates.
28. Most PAC funds go to _____ congressmen.

Knowledge Objective: To understand the 2002 campaign finance reform legislation
29. Arizona Senator _____ _____ was one of the major forces behind the 2002 campaign finance reform legislation.
30. The scandal associated with the collapse of the energy corporation _____ helped to accelerate passage of the legislation.
31. The 2002 law _____ (does, doesn't) allow public financing of congressional elections.
32. _____ money was unregulated money that went for party-building activities.

PART IV — POST-TEST

1. James Madison urged the control of contending factions under the new constitution in an essay called
   - a. Failing Factions.
   - b. Letters of the Federal Farmer.
   - c. Downing #9.
   - d. Federalist #10.

2. Many of the strongest "unions" in terms of their political effectiveness are _____ organizations.
   - a. recreational
   - b. racial
   - c. feminine
   - d. professional

3. Those organizations that insist that they are solely devoted to the public welfare are called
   - a. ideological.
   - b. professional.
   - c. public interest.
   - d. political.

4. One of the following factors is normally not critical in determining a group's political strength.
   - a. strong leadership
   - b. size of membership
   - c. unity of membership
   - d. geographical distribution

5. Ralph Nader, the American Civil Liberties Union, and the NAACP have depended heavily upon _____ to influence public policy.
   - a. litigation
   - b. direct action
   - c. persuasion
   - d. campaign spending

6. The political arm of a business/labor/professional interest group is called a
   - a. LEG.
   - b. GYP.
   - c. CON.
   - d. PAC.

7. The least important factor in determining the support of candidates by business PACs is their
   - a. voting record.
   - b. incumbency.
   - c. winability.
   - d. party affiliation.

8. The Lobbying Disclosure Act of 1995 did all but one of the following.
   - a. reformed campaign finances
   - b. expanded the definition of a lobbyist
   - c. increased disclosure requirements
   - d. required lawyer-lobbyists for foreign entities to register

9. When a group finds the normal political processes closed, they are apt to turn to
   - a. propaganda.
   - b. rule-making.
   - c. litigation.
   - d. persuasion.

10. According to the 2002 law, how much can an individual contribute to a federal candidate in the general election?
    - a. $1000
    - b. $2000
    - c. $3000
    - d. $4000

PART V — TEST ANSWERS

Pretest

1.	a		6.	d
2.	d		7.	d
3.	c		8.	d
4.	a		9.	b
5.	a		10.	b

Programmed Review

1. *Federalist* # 10
2. factions
3. interest
4. values
5. conscience
6. labor unions
7. special interests
8. occupational
9. American Farm Bureau AFL-CIO; U.S. Chamber of Commerce
10. public interest
11. Ralph Nader
12. ideological
13. Single interest
14. size, involvement
15. overlapping
16. incentives
17. litigation
18. cooperative
19. *Register*
20. revolving door
21. specialized knowledge
22. PACs
23. business
24. do not
25. COPE
26. bundle
27. Party
28. incumbent
29. McCain
30. Enron
31. doesn't
32. Soft

Post-test

1.	d		6.	d
2.	d		7.	d
3.	c		8.	a
4.	b		9.	c
5.	a		10.	b

Chapter 7
Political Parties: Essential To Democracy

PART I — GUIDEPOSTS

1. What Parties Do for Democracy
   a. What are the major functions of parties? Evaluate their performance in each category.
   b. What three methods have been used by parties to select candidates? Which method is the most common today?
   c. Are political parties an appropriate vehicle for social reform?
   d. What is the role of third parties?
   e. What contributions to American government have third parties made?
   f. Why do third parties usually fail? What are the two types of third parties?

2. A Brief History of American Political Parties
   a. What was the attitude of the Founding Fathers toward parties? Why?
   b. What were the original names of the Democratic party?
   c. What party emerged to replace the Federalists?
   d. How was the spoils system used by political parties?
   e. What were the origins of the GOP?
   f. How did reforms of the Progressive Era affect political parties?
   g. What groups were brought together in FDR's New Deal?
   h. In what sense were attempts of Reagan to make Republicans the dominant party thwarted?
   i. What are four examples of "realigning elections"?
   j. Why do we have "divided government" today, especially after 2000?
   k. How did the 2002 election depart from historic patterns?

3. American Parties Today
   a. What characteristics do both major parties share today?
   b. How do Americans view political parties today?
   c. How are parties organized at the national level? Describe the role of the presidential convention, the national committee, the national party chairperson, and party platforms.
   d. What is the role of congressional and senatorial campaign committees?
   e. How are parties organized at the state, county, and local level?
   f. How do political parties operate in the Congress; executive branch; judicial branch, state and local governments?
   g. What distinctions have existed historically between Democrats and Republicans? How do they differ today?
   h. What are the different ways citizens view party partisanship?
   i. How important is party identification?

4. Are Political Parties "Dying"?/2002 Campaign Finance Reform Legislation
   a. What is meant by party realignment? What prospects confront each party in the new century? What are party unity scores?
   b. What three charges are leveled against the parties?
   c. What procedural reforms have been adopted by Democrats? Republicans?
   d. How did soft money affect the 1998, 2000, and 2002 elections?
   e. Review the many "effects" of the 2002 campaign finance reform law.
   f. Why may soft money donors now contribute to issue advocacy groups?
   g. What impact did Enron have upon the passage of the 2002 legislation?

PART II — PRETEST

1. The percentage of party members who vote together on roll call votes is called
   a. patronage.
   b. party unity scores.
   c. proportionality.
   d. dealignment.

2. Managing the presidential campaign is the job of
   a. the national committee.
   b. the national chairman.
   c. the attorney general.
   d. the presidential press secretary.

3. The first Republican party was led by
   a. Jefferson.
   b. Hamilton
   c. Washington.
   d. Adams.

4. Candidates are selected by their parties because of
   a. party loyalty.
   b. personal appeal.
   c. endorsement by party leaders.
   d. ideological correctness.

5. When voters may choose what ballot they will vote in a primary, it is called
   a. closed.
   b. open.
   c. realignment.
   d. dealignment.

6. The purpose of a political party is
   a. to recruit potential officeholders.
   b. to simplify alternatives.
   c. to unite the electorate.
   d. all of the above.

7. A striking characteristic of third parties is that they
   a. advance controversial issues and ideas.
   b. are always radical.
   c. are always conservative.
   d. have no place in the American system.

8. The most significant factor influencing the character of American political parties is
   a. the federal system.
   c. the party seniority system.

b. the national convention.   d. the presidential primary.

9. Which of the following is not a present-day function of political parties?
   a. distribution of welfare handouts
   b. stimulation of interest in public affairs
   c. recruitment of political leadership
   d. linkage between the mass public and government

10. A major cause for the persistence of the two-party system in the United States is that
    a. the major parties have become disciplined and issue-oriented.
    b. election districts have a single incumbent.
    c. third parties have failed to point up issues.
    d. major party ideas and platform are too much like religious dogma.

PART III — PROGRAMMED REVIEW

Knowledge objective: To analyze what parties do for democracy
1. Parties organize the _____ by choosing candidates to run under their label.
2. Parties failed to unify the electorate in the 1860s over the issue of _____.
3. Politicians are nominated largely on the basis of their qualifications and personal appeal, not _____ loyalty.
4. The outcomes of American elections (do, do not) _____ make a difference in public policy.
5. Party _____ include simplifying issues, stimulating interest, uniting different segments of society, and recruiting political leadership.
6. Political parties formerly served as a kind of employment agency through their control of _____.
7. As a method of choosing candidates, the caucus was replaced by party _____ which on the state level were replaced by the _____.
8. The American two-party system is maintained because in our single election districts only _____ candidate wins.
9. Third parties organize around a _____ or an _____.

Knowledge Objective: To review the long history of American political parties
10. The Federalist party was challenged by the first _____ party, headed by Jefferson.
11. Today's _____ party (Grand Old Party) arose out of the Civil War.
12. _____ created a party coalition of Southerners, labor, farmers, the unemployed and suburbanites.
13. Until the 1994 midterm elections, Republicans have been more successful in winning _____ elections than congressional elections.

Knowledge Objective: To review the present state of our parties
14. Modern political parties have (more, less) _____ voice in choosing presidential candidates.

15. Both parties today are (moderate, sharply different) _____ in policies and leadership.
16. Political parties in the United States are primarily organized to win political _____.
17. The reason why political parties are so decentralized is the _____ basis of our government.
18. In recent years the party's national committee has given the state and county organizations _____ money.
19. The supreme authority in both political parties is the national _____ convention.
20. A national_____ heads each of the two major parties.
21. Party platforms try to _____ differences in order to appeal to as many voters as possible.
22. In the U.S. Congress, the committee chairs of all the standing committees come from the _____ party.
23. Democrats are (more/less) _____ likely than Republicans to give government a large role in social-economic programs.
24. Today the party remains an important consideration in the naming of _____ judges.
25. A _____ primary is one in which voters are restricted to a single party in the primary election.
26. Party _____ is the single best predictor of the voter.
27. Efforts to reshuffle existing political coalitions is called _____.
28. Pure _____ are the least apt to vote.
29. The main charges against political parties is failure to take meaningful stands on _____ and weak _____.
30. The technology that has had the most impact on elections is the _____.

Knowledge Objective: Discuss "Can parties be saved?"; Campaign Finance, 2002
31. One reform by the GOP was to give ____ ____ more control over presidential races.
32. Democrats created "_____" positions for elected officials/party leaders.
33. Soft money donors may contribute to _____ _____ groups in the future.
34. According to 2002, a deduction up to _____ can go to party committees.

PART IV — POST-TEST

1. The person least likely to vote is a
   a. strong Democrat.
   b. weak Republican.
   c. pure Independent.
   d. middle-of-the-road Democrat.

2. The _____ party evolved out of the crisis over slavery.
   a. Whig
   b. Democratic
   c. Modern Republican
   d. Second Federalist

3. Third-party leaders have included all of the following except

a. Ralph Nader.
c. George Wallace.
b. Ross Perot.
d. Governor Jerry Brown.

4. In both major parties, the supreme authority is the
    a. candidate.
    c. national nominating convention.
    b. party chairman.
    d. primaries.

5. The grass roots of each party is
    a. in the deep south.
    b. in the western states.
    c. at the city, town, ward, and precinct level.
    d. at the family, church, and school level.

6. The party that put together a grand coalition lasting from the Civil War until 1932
   was
    a. Democratic.
    c. Whigs.
    b. Republican.
    d. none of the above.

7. Under the dealignment theory, people have
    a. become Reagan Democrats.
    b. become presidential Democrats.
    c. abandoned both parties to become Independents.
    d. returned to liberal Democrats.

8. When a voter must be registered in a party to vote in the primary, it is called
    a. closed.
    c. direct.
    b. open.
    d. crossover.

9. Republicans in the past decade have not emphasized one of the following reforms.
    a. membership recruitment
    c. grassroots organization
    b. racial and sex quotas
    d. candidate training programs

10. Both major political parties today are
    a. relatively weak.
    c. class-oriented.
    b. strong coalitions.
    d. tightly disciplined.

PART V — TEST ANSWERS

Pretest

1.	b	6.	d
2.	b	7.	a
3.	a	8.	a
4.	b	9.	a
5.	b	10.	b

Programmed Review

1. competition
2. slavery
3. party
4. do
5. functions
6. patronage
7. conventions; primaries
8. one
9. candidate, ideology
10. Republican
11. Republican
12. FDR
13. presidential
14. less
15. moderate
16. power
17. federal
18. soft
19. party
20. committee
21. conceal
22. majority
23. more
24. federal
25. closed
26. identification
27. realignment
28. independents
29. issues, organization
30. television
31. national committee
32. superdelegates
33. Issue advocacy
34. 10,000

Post-test

1. c
2. c
3. d
4. c
5. c
6. b
7. c
8. a
9. b
10. a

Chapter 8
Public Opinion, Participation, and Voting

PART I—GUIDEPOSTS

1. Introduction/Public Opinion
   a. What is public opinion?
   b. What is meant by intensity, latency, and salience as applied to public opinion?
   c. How was the "canvass process" used in the 2000 election?
   d. What is the meaning of polarization?
   e. Why is proper sampling based upon randomness? Also, how do the poll questions—wording, type, etc.—influence poll results?
   f. How did the Republican STOMP program mobilize voters in 2002?

2. Political Socialization
   a. How influential is your family in shaping your political attitudes?
   b. What institution ranks next to the family?
   c. What happens if a young person has a conflict between parents and friends?
   d. Why is the mass media (especially TV) important?
   e. Why are religion and ethnic background important?
   f. Why do adults sometimes shift their childhood attitudes?
   g. Name an issue about which there is general consensus.
   h. How do the attentive public and part-time citizens differ?
   i. According to the Putnam study, how did civic attitudes/behavior change after the terrorist attacks of 9/11? Also, how did 9/11 change U.S. patriotism?

3. Participation: Translating Opinions into Action
   a. How can a citizen participate in government other than voting?
   b. Why is politics mostly a private activity for most Americans?
   c. In which election is voter turnout the greatest and the lowest?
   d. How can voting laws affect voting rates?
   e. How have eligibility standards for voting been expanded by legislation and constitutional amendments?
   f. Why and how is registration important to political participation?
   g. How does one explain the surge in 2000 voting by African Americans?

4. Nonvoting: Who and Why?
   a. What are the causes of low turnout?
   b. Is nonvoting a serious problem?
   c. What are the characteristics of nonvoters?
   d. How can the barriers to nonvoting be reduced?
   e. What are the demographic characteristics of those who vote?
   f. How does social status impact on voting behavior?
   g. Which specific electoral reforms were proposed after the 2000 election?

h. Would Internet voting and voting by mail increase turnout—why or why not?

5. Voting Choices
    a. How does partisanship identification differ from party registration?
    b. Who are the independents? How do they differ from partisans?
    c. What are the positive aspects of candidate appeal? Give examples of candidates with positive appeal, negative appeal. Use the Gore-Bush 2000 race.
    d. How important are issues in determining how a person votes?
    e. How does the U.S. compare to other countries in the categories of registration and voting?

PART II — PRETEST

1. Nonvoters do not have one of the following characteristics.
    a. poor   c. less religious
    b. less educated   d. less white

2. Public opinion is best thought of as
    a. the will of the people.
    b. a diversity of opinion within a particular population.
    c. media reflection of public attitudes.
    d. voter attitudes.

3. An institutional barrier that blocks people from voting is
    a. distant voting booths.   c. unattractive candidates.
    b. registration.   d. lack of party competition.

4. The group least apt to vote is
    a. 18- to 24-year-olds.   c. blue-collar workers.
    b. Gray Panthers.   d. women.

5. The most homogeneous of all groups in molding political opinion is
    a. school.   c. church membership.
    b. work.   d. family.

6. Which of the following was most apt to vote Democratic in recent elections?
    a. Jews   c. white Protestants
    b. blacks   d. Catholics

7. The major force in the early socialization of children is
    a. television.   c. school.
    b. family.   d. playmates.

8. The most influential factor in forming the attitudes of children is
    a. intelligence.   c. class and race.
    b. psychological and genetic traits.   d. family and school.

9. Which group tends to be more liberal on both economic/non-economic issues?
   a. Catholic
   b. Jewish
   c. atheist
   d. Protestant

10. In 2002, both parties were launching major efforts to register/mobilize voters for 2004 from which rapidly-growing ethnic or racial group?
    a. Asian Americans
    b. African Americans
    c. Hispanics
    d. Arab Americans

PART III — PROGRAMMED REVIEW

Knowledge Objective: To consider the complexity of public opinion
1. The people speak with many voices. There is no one set _____ _____.
2. The characteristic of public opinion that measures how strongly people feel on an issue is called _____.
3. _____ attitudes are dormant but may be evoked into action.
4. Opinions which are closely associated with the lives of the individuals are called _____.
5. When a large majority of voters agree on an issue, we have reached _____.
6. When strong opinions are nearly equally divided on an issue, the result is _____.

Knowledge Objective: To examine how we acquire our political attitudes
7. The _____ unit instills the basic attitudes that shape future opinions.
8. The process by which we develop our political attitudes is called political _____.
9. The attitudes of children are shaped by their family _____.
10. After 9/11, many Americans turned their attention to _____ fundamentalism.
11. One should avoid _____ when talking about racial or religious voting.

Knowledge Objective: To examine the practice of "taking the pulse of the people"
12. An accurate poll must be based on a _____ sample of the total universe.
13. Plus or minus 3 percentage points refers to a poll's margin of _____.

Knowledge Objective: To identify those who vote and those who do not
14. The type of political activity most Americans engage in is _____.
15. A subset of the public that has a high level of political interest and awareness is the _____ public.
16. In recent presidential elections, about (half, three-quarters) _____ of potential voters cast ballots.
17. Compared to other nations, voting participation by Americans is (low, high) _____.
18. Millions of Americans fail to vote because they feel there is no real _____.
19. The key factor that determines the degree of voting participation is _____.
20. Persons in the 18-24 age group have the (highest, lowest) _____ voting participation record.
21. Highly educated people are (more, less) _____ apt to vote.

43

22. The major institutional block to voting is _____.
23. In an effort to attract young voters, Congress passed the _____ _____ law.

Knowledge Objective: To determine the patterns of American voting

24. Nonvoting on the part of the _____ is a part of a larger political-psychological environment that discourages their political activity.
25. The _____ has the greatest influence in determining a person's voting patterns and party allegiance.
26. The best indicator of how a person will vote is _____ identification.
27. More than a third of the voters can be called _____.
28. Recent elections marked a focus from parties to _____.
29. Low-income voters tend to judge a candidate (more/less) _____ on the basis of their own personal financial condition.
30. A person's subjective sense of political identification is called _____.
31. Outranking issues or political ideology is _____ identification.
32. Most presidential candidates (do, do not) _____ clearly define their attitudes on issues.

PART IV — POST-TEST

1. The Bush presidential quality that mattered most to voters in 2000 was
   a. strong leadership.
   b. caring about people.
   c. honesty.
   d. understanding issues.

2. One of the following is not a reason why low-income people vote in fewer numbers.
   a. They have less sense of involvement and confidence.
   b. They feel at a disadvantage in social contacts.
   c. Their social norms tend to deemphasize politics.
   d. They can't afford registration fees.

3. All of the following are true about voter statistics except
   a. men out-vote women by a large majority.
   b. middle-aged people are more likely to vote than younger people.
   c. college-educated persons vote more than high school graduates.
   d. persons who are active in organized groups are more likely to vote.

4. An off-year election is one in which
   a. the president is running for reelection.
   b. governors are selected.
   c. senators are selected.
   d. local officials are selected.

5. Candidates with positive appeal include all but
   a. Eisenhower.
   b. Kennedy.
   c. Carter.
   d. Reagan.

6. Voters tend to vote against an incumbent if
   a. the budget is out of balance.
   b. there is an issue conflict.
   c. their personal fortunes are declining.
   d. they have not implemented their campaign promises.

7. In 2002, one-in-four voters declared that their vote was based on which issue(s)?
   a. the war in Afghanistan   c. ethics in government
   b. terrorism and civil liberties   d. jobs and the economy

8. Voter registration procedures have been eased by connecting registration to
   a. college registration.   c. a driver's license.
   b. email.   d. W-4 forms.

9. A good public opinion poll does not require
   a. qualified interviewers.
   b. carefully phrased questions.
   c. a 25 percent sample of the universe.
   d. a representative sample of the universe.

10. One famous presidential election that the Gallup Poll got wrong was in the year
    a. 1948.   c. 1984.
    b. 1960.   d. none of these.

PART V — TEST ANSWERS

Pretest

1.	c	6.	b
2.	b	7.	b
3.	b	8.	d
4.	a	9.	d
5.	d	10.	c

Programmed Review

1.	public opinion	17.	low
2.	intensity	18.	choice
3.	Latent	19.	education
4.	salient	20.	lowest
5.	consensus	21.	more
6.	polarization	22.	registration
7.	family	23.	Motor voter

8. socialization
9. environment
10. Islamic
11. stereotype
12. random
13. error
14. voting
15. attentive
16. half

24. poor
25. family
26. party
27. independent
28. candidates
29. more
30. partisanship
31. partisan
32. do not

Post-test

1. c
2. d
3. a
4. d
5. c

6. c
7. d
8. c
9. c
10. a

Chapter 9
Campaigns and Elections: Democracy in Action

PART I — GUIDEPOSTS

1. The Rules of the Game
   a. Who determines the rules for U.S. elections?
   b. When are elections held in the United States?
   c. Explain: fixed term, staggered term, and term limitation.
   d. What effect does the winner-take-all rule have on our elections?
   e. What is the electoral college? How important is it?
   f. What are the pros/cons of proportional representation?

2. Running for Office
   a. Why do campaigns for Congress vary so widely?
   b. What are some similarities between campaigns for the House and the Senate?
   c. How is the election process distorted today?
   d. How does an emphasis on personality and negative campaigning detract from the true issues?
   e. What is the recent success rate of representatives who run for reelection? Why do critics say we are electing "representatives for life"?
   f. Why must most representatives build a personal rather than a party organization.
   g. What advantages do incumbents have in running for reelection?
   h. Does a big budget assure election to the House?
   i. Why are Senate races more difficult to win?
   j. Why are Senate races of the future less apt to favor incumbents?
   k. Does negative campaigning seem to be effective?
   l. What strategies did the GOP follow in the 2002 election?

3. Running for the President
   a. How are most delegates to the national convention selected?
   b. Why do Iowa and New Hampshire loom so large in the delegate selection process?
   c. How have recent conventions been decided in advance?
   d. Of what value is the party platform?
   e. How is the candidate for vice president selected?
   f. Why do parties continue to have conventions?
   g. How do you run for president of the United States without political party backing?
   h. What factors are considered by candidates in planning their fall campaigns?
   i. How do campaigns resemble marathons?
   j. What is the impact of presidential debates?

4. Improving Elections
   a. What advantages are claimed for the party primary system?
   b. What are the alleged disadvantages?
   c. Why might a national primary be better?
   d. Might national caucuses be better?
   e. Should direct election of the president be substituted for the electoral college?
   f. Is reform of the electoral college likely?

g.   How can the voting process be reformed? What is "e-voting"?

5.   Money in U.S. Elections/2002 Campaign Finance Reform Legislation
   a.   Cite the major scandals involving campaign money.
   b.   Why do the costs of campaigns continue to rise?
   c.   Why is PAC money so controversial?
   d.   How do we now finance presidential campaigns?
   e   Why was so much soft money spent in the 2002 election?
   f.   What is issue advocacy advertising? Why were these ads popular in 2002,
        especially among senior groups? How did the 2002 reforms constrain the ads?
   g.   Why have restrictions on campaign spending not been extended to congressional races?
   h.   What were some criticisms of the FECA?
   i.   What was accomplished by federal finance reform legislation?
   j.   Why is bipartisan campaign finance reform so difficult to achieve?

PART II — PRETEST

1. The most important factor in winning a congressional race is
    a. personal contact.   c. press coverage.
    b. TV time.   d. money.

2. Recent presidential conventions have been noteworthy because
    a. the winner was known in advance.
    b. major rivals made a down-to-the-wire finish.
    c. excitement ran high.
    d. philosophical differences were deep.

3. The political strength of congressional incumbents has made modern elections
    a. highly competitive.   c. uncompetitive.
    b. political party contests.   d. strictly rational contests.

4. The campaign reform law of 1974 was chiefly concerned with
    a. campaign finance.   c. nomination procedures.
    b. media coverage.   d. delegate selection.

5. To attain the presidency, a candidate must achieve two goals. These are
    a. have the largest number of delegates prior to coming to the national convention, and
        then obtain a majority of the popular vote.
    b. be nominated at the party convention, and obtain a majority of the electoral votes.
    c. be nominated at the party convention, and obtain both a majority of the popular vote
        and the electoral vote.
    d. be nominated at the party convention, and win a majority of the popular vote.

6. A recent movement for change in the electoral system has pushed for
    a. fixed terms.   c. term limitations.
    b. staggered terms.   d. uniform terms.

7. A general criticism of the 1988 presidential campaign was that it had

a. erotic symbols. c. negative advertising.
b. no debates. d. ethnic slurs.

8. In the event that no presidential candidate receives a majority of the electoral vote, the president is chosen by
   a. Congress. c. House of Representatives.
   b. Supreme Court. d. Senate.

9. The 2002 legislation raised the individual contribution limit to a candidate in the two year campaign cycle to _____ dollars.
   a. 4000 c. 2000
   b. 3000 d. 1000

10. The largest item in recent congressional campaigns has been for
    a. TV-radio advertising. c. polls.
    b. consultants. d. printing and mailing.

PART III — PROGRAMMED PREVIEW

Knowledge objective: To review the rules for elections
1. Most electoral rules are still matters of _____ law.
2. Federal general elections are the first Tuesday after the first _____ in November of _____ numbered years.
3. Politicians can plan for the next election because we have _____ terms.
4. A recent movement wants to _____ terms of office.
5. Politicians who announce they will not run again are called _____ _____.
6. With our winner-take-all system a winner does not necessarily need to have a _____ of the vote.
7. Proportional representation rewards _____ parties.
8. To win the presidency, the candidate must have a majority vote of the _____ _____.
9. Under the electoral college system, a candidate either wins _____ or _____ of a state's electoral votes.
10. Most states provide for the selection of electors on a (state, district) _____ basis.
11. If no presidential candidate secures a majority of the electoral votes the _____ _____ _____ decides.

Knowledge Objective: To examine the process of running for Congress
12. Competitiveness in congressional elections (has, has not) _____ increased slightly over the past twenty years.
13. Senate elections are likely to be (more, less) _____ competitive than House elections.
14. Congressional candidates whose vote is increased by a strong presidential candidate are said to benefit from the _____ influence.
15. New campaign technology tends to emphasize _____ over issues.
16. Keeping a House seat is (easier, harder) _____ than gaining one.
17. In midterm elections support for the party in power almost always _____.
18. Candidates for Congress secure most of their campaign funds from (the party, personal contributions) _____.
19. Focusing on an opponent's failings is _____ campaigning.

Knowledge Objective: To trace the steps in nominating and electing a president

20. Presidential candidates are now selected by their parties chiefly through the use of _____.
21. When voters in a presidential primary indicate their preference from a list of candidates, the election is commonly referred to as a _____ contest.
22. National conventions normally select a party candidate for president and vice president and write a _____.
23. The party platform is (binding, non-binding) _____ on the candidate.
24. Nominating conventions provide a time to build party _____.
25. Mistakes made during a presidential debate may damage the candidate's _____.

Knowledge Objective: To study proposed reforms of the electoral college and presidential primaries

26. In caucus states, candidates are less dependent on the _____ and more dependent on their abilities to reach _____ activists.
27. Reform of presidential primaries concentrates on _____ or a _____ primary.
28. The main argument for presidential primaries is that they open up the nomination process to _____ voters.
29. Critics contend the primaries test the candidate for the ability to play the _____ _____.
30. The most common electoral college reform is _____ _____ _____ of the president.

Knowledge Objective: To analyze the sources/uses of money in national campaigns

31. The Keating 5 is an example of the undue influence that comes with large _____.
32. All congressional candidates (are, are not) _____ required to report their campaign contributions and expenditures.
33. FECA election regulations are being undermined by _____ money.
34. The key to congressional campaigns are _____.
35. Organizations and individuals (do, do not) _____ have limitations placed on the amount they may spend independently of a campaign organization.
36. Congressional candidates (do, do not) _____ receive federal campaign funds.
37. The 2002 campaign finance reform law does not constrain _____ expenditures by groups/individuals separately from political candidates.
38. The 1974 campaign reform law achieved a breakthrough by providing for public _____ of presidential campaigns.
39. The 2002 reforms _____ (did, did not) address incumbent fund-raising advantages.
40. The 2002 campaign finance reform law bans broadcast ads that show the _____ or _____ of a candidate and occurs in _____ days before a general election.

PART IV — POST-TEST

1. Only one of the following presidential candidates was elected, although each received more popular votes than his opponent.
   a. Jackson (1824)
   b. Cleveland (1888)
   c. Tilden (1876)
   d. Truman (1948)

2. The bias of the electoral college favors
   a. one-party states.
   c. populous urban states.

b. rural areas. d. modified one-party states.

3. A state's electoral vote is determined by
   a. population.
   b. previous voting patterns in presidential elections.
   c. a complicated formula devised by Congress.
   d. the number of its representatives and senators.

4. The Supreme Court voided which of the following provisions of the 1974 campaign reform law?
   a. limitations on spending   c. public funding of presidential elections
   b. limitations on giving   d. election-day registration

5. To be elected president, a candidate must receive
   a. a plurality of electoral votes.
   b. a majority of electoral votes.
   c. a majority of states as well as electoral votes.
   d. a majority of the popular vote.

6. Most delegates to the national nominating convention are chosen by
   a. popular votes.   c. state conventions.
   b. primary elections.   d. state committees.

7. Presidential candidates are nominated by
   a. party caucus.   c. national party committee.
   b. national party conventions.   d. presidential primary.

8. New candidates for the House of Representatives are normally concerned with
   a. timing.   c. recognition.
   b. financial support. d. all of the above.

9. The 1974 campaign expense law placed a limit on the contributions that could be made by
   a. individuals.   c. political parties.
   b. organizations.   d. all of the above.

10. A "permanent Congress" is a result of
    a. advantages held by incumbents. c. redistricting.
    b. direct mail.   d. direct primaries.

PART V — TEST ANSWERS

Pretest

1.	a	6	c
2.	a	7.	c
3.	c	8.	c
4.	a	9.	a
5.	b	10.	a

1. state
2. Monday; even
3. fixed
4. limit
5. lame duck
6. majority
7. minority
8. electoral college
9. all; none
10. state
11. House of Representatives
12. has not
13. more
14. coattail
15. personality
16. easier
17. declines
18. personal contributions
19. negative
20. primaries
21. beauty
22. platform
23. non-binding
24. unity
25. credibility
26. media; political
27. national; regional
28. more
29. media game
30. direct popular election
31. contributions
32. are
33. soft
34. PACs
35. do not
36. do not
37. independent
38. financing
39. did not
40. image; likeness; 60

Chapter 10
The Media and American Politics

PART I — GUIDEPOSTS

1. The Influence of the Media on Politics
    a. How did the media handle the reporting of the 1996,1998, 2000, 2002 elections?
    b. What is the media's major role in American politics?
    c. How is our culture affected by the mass media?
    d. What new technological changes in the media are emerging?
    e. How are new competitors affecting the established media?
    f. What is the impact of the Internet upon the political process?

2. The Changing Role of the American News Media
    a. How is the role of today's press different from the press of Thomas Jefferson's day?
    b. What is objective journalism?
    c. How did FDR use radio as a political tool?
    d. Where do Americans get most of their news?
    e. Is the mass media a business or a public service industry?
    f. What do journalists believe is their function in elections?
    g. What is the significance of media conglomerates?

3. Mediated Politics
    a. How have the media changed American politics?
    b. What factors determine how a person interprets media messages?
    c. Why do both liberals and conservatives feel the media is biased?
    d. Why is the media's role in setting the national agenda so important?

4. The Media and Elections
    a. How has modern media changed political campaigns? What are negative ads?
    b. How do media consultants differ from political party advisers?
    c. Why does the media often picture campaigns as a "horse race"?
    d. Do voters make their decisions on the basis of media reporting?
    e. How does the reporting of election results influence elections?
    f. Why do many candidates now have their own Web pages?
    g. What are "focus groups"?

5. Media and Governance
    a. What is the media's role in the policy process?
    b. What has been the relationship of recent presidents with the press?
    c. Why has Congress suffered at the hands of the press?
    d. Why is the Supreme Court the least dependent upon the press?
    e. Is the claim "the media is the fourth branch of the government" exaggerated?

PART II — PRETEST

1. Freedom of the press is guaranteed by
    a. American tradition.
    b. common law.
    c. Congress.
    d. a constitutional amendment.

2. One of the following media powers is normally not included in the top national ranking.
    a. *Reader's Digest*
    b. *ABC*
    c. *Wall Street Journal*
    d. *USA Today*

3. The media's new form of a town meeting is
    a. 60 minutes.
    b. computer voting.
    c. Web chat rooms.
    d. soundbites.

4. The network semi-monopoly over television has been _____ by C-SPAN and CNN.
    a. reinforced
    b. diminished
    c. untouched
    d. overshadowed

5. The media during a presidential election tends not to stress
    a. issues.
    b. personalities.
    c. strategy.
    d. the race.

6. Recent studies of the media's political reporting tend to be critical of their
    a. partisan bias.
    b. skimpy political coverage.
    c. repetitive coverage of issues.
    d. treatment of the election as a contest.

7. Which of the following has not become a national newspaper?
    a. *Atlanta Constitution*
    b. *USA Today*
    c. *Wall Street Journal*
    d. *New York Times*

8. The most trusted source of news is
    a. newspapers.

b. news magazines.

c. radio.

d. television.

9. The president who has been most successful in using television to further his goals has been
    a. Kennedy.
    b. Eisenhower.
    c. Franklin Roosevelt.
    d. Reagan.

10. The mass media's impact on most Americans is modified by their
    a. regionalism.
    b. viewing habits.
    c. lack of background.
    d. selective perception.

PART III — PROGRAMMED REVIEW

Knowledge Objective: To evaluate the power of the mass media

1. In modern America the mass media is so powerful that it is sometimes called the _____ _____ of government.
2. Recent expansion of news sources has resulted in more competition for _____.
3. The _____ media is the part of the mass media that stresses the news.
4. The early American press served as a political _____ for political leaders.
5. Professional journalists believe the journalists should be _____ of partisan politics.
6. FDR effectively used the radio to _____ the editorial screening of the press.
7. Today _____ is the most important source of news for most Americans.
8. Media conglomerates now dominate the media business and have contributed to the _____ of news.
9. Critics charge that information today is more diluted and moderated because local TV and newspapers are not owned by _____ firms.
10. The _____ , not political parties, are now judging candidates in terms of character.

Knowledge Objective: To examine the relationship of the media and public opinion

11. For a long time political scientists have tended to (stress, play down) _____ the mass media's political influence.
12. Defense mechanisms such as _____ perception modify the influence of the mass media.
13. A powerful check on media as an opinion-making force is _____ _____.
14. Much of the media's opinion-making role is (direct, indirect) _____.
15. The final decision in determining the public agenda (is, is not) _____ made by the media.
16. _____ complain that the media are too liberal, and the liberals claim the media are too _____.
17. David Broder has expressed concern about the _____ of journalists who previously were in government service.

18. Modern presidents have turned away from the press and to _____ and _____ to communicate with the public.
19. In recent decades, newspaper publishers tended to support _____ presidential candidates.
20. Generally, reporters are _____, while publishers take _____ positions.
21. Critics of presidential use of television have called TV a _____.
22. Some critics contend that elite journalists have a _____ bias.
23. Some studies indicate that the liberal bias of reporters (is, is not) _____ reflected in their on-the-job performance.

Knowledge Objective: To evaluate the role of the media in elections
24. The media tend to portray the presidential election as a _____.
25. Public relations experts attached to campaigns tend to stress the candidate's _____.
26. Election experts tend to determine their campaign strategy on the basis of _____.
27. Old-time party leaders have been replaced in presidential campaigns by experts and _____.
28. The broadcast networks now attract only about _____ percent of the viewing public.

Knowledge Objective: To evaluate media power in American politics
29. The press does not pay much attention to policy _____.
30. In evaluating media power, the media scholars (agree, disagree) _____.
31. The news media's greatest role as a participant is probably at the _____ level of government.
32. Lack of coverage of the bureaucracy is due to little interest by the media in reporting policy _____.
33. Most media coverage of Congress is its reaction to initiatives of the _____.
34. Most Americans believe that the media (is, is not) _____ a valuable watchdog over government.

PART IV — POST-TEST

1. In most national elections a majority of newspapers endorse _____ candidates.
    a. conservative
    b. liberal
    c. independent
    d. no

2. Critics of media employees charge that an overwhelming majority are
    a. conservative.
    b. liberal.
    c. independent.
    d. apolitical.

3. The most influential component of today's mass media is
    a. newspapers.
    b. television.
    c. radio.
    d. news magazine

4. In addition to their public service role in providing information, the media also
    a. are privately owned.
    b. are big business.
    c. stress profits.
    d. are all of the above.

5. The modern president who has held the fewest news conferences has been
   a. Carter.   c. Nixon.
   b. Reagan.   d. Johnson.

6. Using entertainment techniques to present the news is called
   a. infotainment.   c. a media event.
   b. internet.   d. an infomercial.

7. Ownership of media outlets is
   a. widely dispersed.   c. unprofitable.
   b. concentrated.   d. family-oriented.

8. The president who held the largest number of press conferences was
   a. John F. Kennedy.
   b. Franklin D. Roosevelt.
   c. Richard M. Nixon.
   d. Lyndon B. Johnson.

9. How citizens interpret information from politicians depends upon all but:
   a. recall ability.   c. hours spent watching television.
   b. political socialization.   d. selectivity.

10. The institution least dependent on the press is the
    a. Supreme Court.   c. bureaucracy.
    b. president.   d. Congress.

PART V — TEST ANSWERS

Pretest

1.	d	6.	d
2.	a	7.	a
3.	c	8.	d
4.	b	9.	d
5.	a	10.	d

Programmed Review

1.	fourth branch	18.	radio, television
2.	newspapers	19.	Republican
3.	news	20.	liberal; conservative
4.	mouthpiece	21.	throne
5.	independent	22.	cultural
6.	bypass	23.	is not

7. television
8. centralization
9. local
10. press
11. play down
12. selective
13. group affiliation
14. indirect
15. is not
16. Conservatives;
    pro-establishment
17. objectivity

24. race
25. image
26. fifty
27. consultants
28. soundbites
29. implementation
30. disagree
31. local
32. implementation
33. President
34. is

Post-test

1. a
2. b
3. b
4. d
5. b

6. a
7. b
8. b
9. c
10. a

Chapter 11
Congress: The People's Branch

PART I — GUIDEPOSTS

1. Congressional Elections
    a. What is meant by a "safe seat"? What is meant by a "swing district"?
    b. How often is redistricting required? What triggers redistricting? How do some groups benefit from gerrymandering? Under what restrictions are congressional district lines drawn?
    c. Why is incumbency an advantage?
    d. What factors influence congressional election outcomes?
    e. Why could excessive partisan gerrymandering be unconstitutional?
    f. Why are Senate campaigns better financed and more competitive than House elections?
    g. What were the key reasons for GOP successes in the 2002 election?

2. The Structure and Powers of Congress
    a. What general powers were given to Congress by the Constitution?
    b. What special powers was it given?
    c. In the national contest for power why has the president gained more than Congress?
    d. How does the U.S. Senate differ from the French Senate or German Bundesrat?
    e. What are the consequences of bicameralism?
    f. How does the impeachment process work?
    g. What are the seven important functions of Congress?

3. Managing Congress
    a. Why was the legislative branch originally divided into two parts?
    b. How has the House of Representatives made its procedures more efficient?
    c. What special powers does the Speaker have? How was Gingrich a different Speaker? Why did he eventually resign?
    d. What other officers supplement the Speaker's leadership?
    e. What key role is played by the House Rules Committee?
    f. What official dominates Senate procedure? What is "senatorial courtesy"?
    g. What has been the trend with regard to power of the Senate establishment? Why did Senate Majority Leader Trent Lott resign his position in 2002? Who is Senator Bill Frist?
    h. How have Senate minorities used the filibuster? How can cloture be used to end filibusters? Also, what is meant by the "hold" practice?
    i. Why have confirmations by the Senate become more political?
    j. What are some of the major differences between the House and Senate?
    k. What is the difference between judicial and administrative appointments?

4. The Job of Legislator/The Legislative Obstacle Course
    a. Why is the job of a legislator so hectic? Also, how has the "face of Congress" changed? What are the policy consequences of those changes?
    b. What is the *delegate* theory of representation? The *trustee* theory? Who is apt to hold each view?

c. What role do each of the following play in a congressman's voting record: ideology; voter opinion; colleagues; staff; party; president; seniority; other influences?
d. What are the obstacles to legislative action? Why is compromise so important?
e. Explain the following: standing committees, riders, mark-up, veto, and pocket veto.
f. What is the difference between authorization and appropriation?

5. Committees: The Little Legislatures?
   a. Why is Congress sometimes called a collection of committees?
   b. How are committee members selected?
   c. How important are the chairs of committees and subcommittees?
   d. What role does seniority play in committees?
   e. How valuable are committee investigations and oversight activities?
   f. How important are conference committees/caucuses?
   g. How do committees develop legislative expertise?

6. Congress: An Assessment and a View on Reform
   a. What are the most frequent criticisms of Congress?
   b. Evaluate each criticism.
   c. In what sense is Congress acting as the Founders anticipated?
   d. How can Congress be defended?

PART II — PRETEST

1. All of the following are true about the House of Representatives except
   a. legislators in the House have two year terms.
   b. there are 435 members in the House.
   c. policy specialists are common in the House.
   d. a filibuster is common in the House.

2. Gerrymandering occurs when the majority party
   a. supports benefits for blue-collar workers.
   b. promises to promote legislation for certain districts.
   c. draws district lines to win as many districts as possible.
   d. draws district lines to maximize its popular vote.

3. Authorization of a program by Congress means nothing until
   a. OMB submits a budget.
   b. the Rules Committee reaches agreement.
   c. the legislative session ends.
   d. Congress appropriates funds.

4. The chief responsibility of congressional staff is to
   a. handle constituent mail.
   b. serve as receptionists.
   c. schedule office appointments.
   d. advise on legislation.

5. Congress does not perform one of these functions.
   a. policy clarification
   b. consensus building
   c. foreign policy initiatives
   d. lawmaking

6. The Speaker of the House of Representatives does all of the following *except*
   - a. grants recognition to a member.
   - b. appoints select and conference committees.
   - c. controls committee assignments.
   - d. directs general business on the floor.

7. In the Senate, the committee responsible for each party's overall legislative program is called the _____ committee.
   - a. policy
   - b. direction
   - c. strategy
   - d. ways-and-means

8. Legislators who base their votes on their analysis of the long-run welfare of the nation are playing a _____ role.
   - a. delegate
   - b. trustee
   - c. pragmatic
   - d. pollster's

9. The seniority system is respected for all but one of the following reasons.
   - a. encourages members to stay on a committee
   - b. encourages expertise
   - c. assures aggressiveness and risk taking
   - d. reduces interpersonal politics

10. Critics of Congress do not commonly complain that it is
    - a. inefficient.
    - b. unrepresentative.
    - c. dominated by the President.
    - d. independent of lobbyists.

PART III — PROGRAMMED REVIEW

Knowledge objective: To review the system for election to Congress and to profile those elected
   1. Redrawing the district lines of U.S. Representatives after each census is the responsibility of _____ _____.
   2. _____ is the process of drawing electoral boundaries to maximize the majority party's house majority.
   3. Being an incumbent is a(n) _____ for a member of Congress seeking reelection.
   4. In 1995 the Supreme Court ruled that making race "the predominant factor" while ignoring traditional principles was _____.
   5. A _____ seat is one that is predictably won by one party.
   6. Nearly half of the legislators are _____ by profession.

Knowledge Objective: To analyze the structure and powers of the houses of Congress
   7. The Framers designed the _____ to reflect the popular will and the _____ to provide stability.
   8. The _____ holds the place in government the Framers intended for Congress.
   9. Congress has the power to declare _____.
   10. The Senate is chaired by a _____ _____ _____ in the absence of the vice president.
   11. Assisting each floor leader are the party _____ who serve as liaisons between the House leadership and the rank-and-file members.
   12. In the Senate, each party has a(n) _____ _____ which is in theory responsible for the party's overall legislative program.

13. The tradition of submitting names of appointees to the senator from the state where the appointee resides is called _____ _____.

14. A filibuster in the Senate can be shut off only by a(n) _____ vote.

15. The Senate has the power to _____ presidential nominations.

Knowledge Objective: To consider the job of the legislator

16. Members of Congress who see their role as _____ believe they should serve the "folks back home."

17. Members of Congress who see their role as _____ are free-thinking legislators who vote their conscience.

18. The main influence on legislators is their perception of how their _____ feel about the matters brought before Congress.

19. Most members of Congress are now highly dependent on their _____ .

Knowledge Objective: To trace the lawmaking process

20. From the very beginning, Congress has been a system of multiple _____ .

21. To follow a bill through the congressional labyrinth is to see the _____ of power in Congress.

22. Proponents of new legislation must win at every step; _____ need win only once.

Knowledge Objective: To examine the committee system

23. All bills introduced in the House are sent to _____ committees.

24. As the power of congressional subcommittees has expanded, the importance of _____ has diminished.

25. _____ are still usually named on the basis of seniority.

26. If neither house will accept the other's bills, a(n) _____ _____ settles the difference.

Knowledge Objective: To examine major criticisms of Congress

27. Critics judge that Congress is _____ because the committee system responds too much to organized regional interests.

28. Congress lacks collective _____ .

29. Congress (has, has not) _____ created ethics committees to monitor the behavior of members.

30. Congress often deals with complex issues for which there is no _____ among members of Congress or the general public.

PART IV — POST-TEST

1. The profile of the 107th Congress would tend to support which assertion?
   a. The vast majority were men.
   c. The average age was 35-40.
   b. There were no women.
   d. none of these

2. Members of Congress from competitive districts are apt to make _____ their first priority.
   a. serving the home folks
   c. national issues
   b. foreign policy
   d. supporting the president

3. Special responsibilities of the Senate *do not include* two of the following.
   a. ratification of treaties
   b. confirmation of presidential nominees

     c. a final veto on appropriations

     d. nomination of ambassadors to foreign countries

4. In terms of the general makeup of Congress, which of the following people would be most typical?

     a. a millionaire Jewish stockbroker

     b. a Catholic steel worker

     c. a Protestant female elementary teacher

     d. a middle-income male lawyer

5. One of the following persons would have the best chance of election to Congress.

     a. an incumbent representative   c. an experienced state legislator

     b. a popular TV anchorperson   d. a famous woman astronaut

6. Free-thinking and independent legislators see their role as

     a. national figures.   c. diplomats.

     b. trustees.   d. ambassadors from localities.

7. The role of the president has become enhanced at the expense of the Congress, especially _____ policy.

     a. domestic   c. economic

     b. foreign   d. social

8. The vast majority of the bills introduced every two years in both chambers are

     a. passed.   c. killed.

     b. still under debate.   d. withdrawn.

9. The majority floor leader is an officer

     a. only of his party.

     b. in charge of both parties in standing and conference committees.

     c. in charge of both parties on the floor.

     d. who presides over the Senate.

10. House party whips do all of the following *except*

     a. serve as liaison between leadership and the rank-and-file.

     b. inform members when important bills will be voted.

     c. lobby strongly for support of the majority leader.

     d. try to ensure maximum attendance for critical votes.

PART V — TEST ANSWERS

Pretest

1.	d	6.	c
2.	c	7.	a
3.	d	8.	b
4.	d	9.	c
5.	c	10.	d

Programmed Review

1. state legislatures
2. gerrymandering
3. advantage
4. unconstitutional
5. safe
6. lawyers
7. House; Senate
8. president
9. war
10. president pro tempore
11. whips
12. policy committee
13. senatorial courtesy
14. cloture
15. confirm

16. delegate
17. trustee
18. constituents
19. staff
20. vetoes
21. dispersion
22. opponents
23. standing
24. seniority
25. Chairpersons
26. conference committee
27. unrepresentative
28. responsibility
29. has
30. consensus

Post-test

1. a
2. a
3. c, d
4. d
5. a

6. b
7. b
8. c
9. a
10. c

64

Chapter 12
The Presidency: The Leadership Branch

PART I — GUIDEPOSTS

1. Introduction/The Structure and Powers of the Presidency
    a. What built-in checks apply to presidential power?
    b. Why did the framers outline the powers of the president in such broad terms? How did the framers define the presidency and presidential ticket?
    c. Why and how has presidential power increased vis-à-vis Congress?
    d. How does divided government impact upon the presidency?
    e. How did President George W. Bush's performance after 9/11 illustrate both the powers of and constraints upon the modern presidency?
    f. What other types of "presidential systems" exist around the world?
    g. What are executive privilege, the "take care clause," inherent powers, and the State of the Union Address?
    h. What is the line of succession to the presidency as established by Congress?
    i. What is the "pardon power"?

2. What Americans Expect of Their Presidents
    a. What are the mixed reactions Americans have to presidential power?
    b. What qualities do we demand of our presidents?
    c. Whom do we rate as our five best presidents? Who are presidential failures?
    d. What are the constitutional qualifications to be president?

3. Roles Assumed by the President/Managing the Presidency
    a. How do presidents perform as "crisis managers" and "morale builders"? Also, explain their roles as recruiters, agenda setters, legislative/political coalition builders, party leaders, and communicators to the public.
    b. Summarize the key areas/policy responsibilities found in the "presidential job description."
    c. In what ways is public attention focused on the presidency?
    d. How can this attention be used to his advantage? Can this attention turn against him?
    e. How does a president's role as ceremonial leader conflict with his partisan political image?
    f. Why can a president's appointments have long-range consequences?
    g. What voice do presidents have in setting national priorities?
    h. Why does the president play a central role in foreign policy?
    i. How does the president's help determine national economic policy?
    j. How do presidents enlist the direct support of the people?
    k. Of what use are State of the Union and written policy addresses?
    l. Why are effective presidents also adroit politicians?
    m. Why do presidents face potential damage if they have poor advisers?
    n. What is meant by the EOP and who composes it? What is the importance of the White House Staff, the Chief of Staff, and OMB?
    o. Why do presidents rarely use the Cabinet as an advisory body?

4. The Vice Presidency/First Lady
   a. Do vice presidents generally perform important functions?
   b. How has the vice presidency been affected by the twenty-second and twenty-fifth Amendments?
   c. How and why are vice presidents subject to the goodwill/mood of the president?
   d. Which vice presidents have played important decision-making roles?
   e. What have been both the traditional/non-traditional roles of the first lady?

5. Holding Presidents Accountable
   a. How can Congress/the courts serve as a check on presidential power?
   b. Why is media coverage of the president normally adversarial?
   c. What role does public opinion play in terms of presidential accountability?
   d. What are "rally points"?
   e. Should presidents be limited to two terms in office--why or why not?

6. Judging Presidential Greatness
   a. What standards are used to judge the effectiveness of presidents?
   b. What have been the qualities of great presidents? Why have presidents failed?
   c. Why are capable advisors so important to presidential success?
   d. Why will it take more time and the judgement of history to assess George W. Bush?

PART II — PRETEST

1. Critics of the presidency seldom charge that it is a(n) _____ institution.
   a. remote, aristocratic
   b. weak, flabby
   c. status quo
   d. Establishment

2. Only one of the following presidents is apt to appear on a list of "greats."
   a. Buchanan
   b. Grant
   c. Truman
   d. Harding

3. The framers of the Constitution did not anticipate presidential _____ _____.
   a. symbolic functions.
   b. abuses of power.
   c. magisterial functions.
   d. legislative role.

4. The Supreme Court decision in *Curtiss v. Wright* (1936) upheld strong presidential authority over
   a. foreign policy.
   b. domestic policy.
   c. budget.
   d. appointments.

5. The constitutionally required age for a president is:.
   a. 35.
   b. 40.
   c. 45.
   d. 50.

6. The important central presidential staff agency that advises the president about hundreds of government agencies is the
    a. Office of Oversight and Investigation.
    b. CIA.
    c. Office of Management and Budget.
    d. GAO.

7. The vice president has not normally been used by modern presidents to
    a. chair advisory councils.
    b. execute day-to-day policy.
    c. undertake good will missions.
    d. serve as a senior advisor.

8. The following persisting paradoxes of the American presidency are true *except* that a president should be
    a. programmatic, but a pragmatic and flexible leader.
    b. a common person who can give an uncommon performance.
    c. a person who delivers more than he or she promises.
    d. above politics, yet a skilled political coalition builder.

9. The fundamental power of the president that can be used to accomplish his goals is
    a. artful deception.
    b. persuasion.
    c. outright deceit.
    d. partisanship.

10. The cabinet secretary who would be last in line to become president handles the Department of
    a. State.
    b. Labor.
    c. Homeland Security.
    d. Defense.

PART III — PROGRAMMED REVIEW

Knowledge Objective: To analyze the characteristics that Americans expect of their president
1. The framers of the Constitution both _____ and _____ centralized leadership.
2. The central characteristic that Americans demand of their president is the quality of _____.
3. In judging presidents, voters rate _____ and _____ over policy decisions.
4. Active presidents are sometimes accused of being _____.

Knowledge Objective: To examine the president's constitutional position
5. The framers created a presidency of _____ powers.
6. The president's power is limited by a system of _____ and _____.
7. The president must be a _____-_____ citizen.
8. Great Britain has a _____ system.

Knowledge Objective: The challenging job of being president and vice president
 9. The principle of _____ control over the military is inherent in U.S. democracy.
 10. The Ethics in Government Act requires _____ of _____ requirements.
 11. Even since the ____ _____, presidents are expected to keep unemployment low.
 12. The vice president casts a tie-breaking vote if there is a tie in the _____.
 13. Presidents must build _____ in order to get the agreement of diverse groups.
 14. Presidents use State of the _____ Addresses.
 15. Presidents use a _____ and _____ organization.

Knowledge Objective: To analyze symbolic leadership
 16. The president's power has been greatly increased by the mass media, especially _____.
 17. The swelling of the presidency in part results from the _____ expectations.
 18. Presidents face a conflict between their role as chief of state and their role as _____ leader.
 19. In acting for all the people, the president is a symbolic leader and _____ of state.

Knowledge Objective: To examine the presidential establishment, constraints on the president, and the issue of presidential accountability
 20. The Supreme Court in the *Curtiss v. Wright* case decided that the president (did, did not) _____ have exclusive powers in the field of international relations.
 21. Since presidents appoint thousands of top officials, one of the chief presidential duties is _____.
 22. Clinton's wife and first lady was the policy activist _____ _____.
 23. For economic policy the president depends on the Secretary of the Treasury, the Council of Economic Advisers, and the Director of the _____.
 24. A president who is a successful leader knows where the _____ are.
 25. George W. Bush relied heavily on his vice president, Dick _____.
 26. To influence media coverage, the president holds _____ _____ .
 27. To gauge public opinion, presidents commission private _____ _____ .
 28. An effective president uses political parties (more, less) _____.
 29. In recent years presidents have come to rely heavily on their personal _____.
 30. The office of _____ and _____ continues to be the central presidential staff agency.
 31. Presidents seldom turn to the _____ as a collective body for advice.
 32. The vice president could serve as "Acting President" under the _____ Amendment.
 33. Australia and Israel have _____ forms of government.
 34. The modern media is the number one _____ of the presidency.
 35. The American people regard television as (more, less) _____ trustworthy than most other American institutions.
 36. President Clinton was criticized for his pardon of refugee commodities broker _____.

Knowledge Objective: To review what constitutes presidential greatness
 37. A president valued more after he left office than when he was president was _____.
 38. One presidential failure was _____ in the 1920s.

PART IV — POST-TEST

1. The American public today gives priority to one aspect of the president.
    a. leadership
    b. honesty
    c. wisdom
    d. policy positions

2. Presidents have the most leeway in
    a. foreign and military affairs.
    b. domestic appropriation matters.
    c. budget appropriations.
    d. social policy.

3. Often a president's "new initiatives" in domestic policy are
    a. highly creative.
    b. previously considered in Congress.
    c. previously thought of by past presidents.
    d. a response to grassroots demands.

4. The functions of the White House staff include *all but*
    a. domestic policy.
    b. economic policy.
    c. congressional relations.
    d. intelligence operations.

5. If the president is to be a successful politician, he must be able to
    a. give commands.
    b. manage conflict.
    c. stand on principles.
    d. rise above politics.

6. Modern presidential cabinets as a collective body have been used by presidents
    a. high-level advisers.
    b. to create a quasi-parliamentary system.
    c. very infrequently.
    d. to assess new policy proposals.

7. Which amendment limits the president to two terms in office?
    a. Twentieth.
    b. Twenty-Second.
    c. Twenty-Fifth.
    d. none of the above

8. Which president was told by the Supreme Court to release steel mills from federal control?
    a. Truman.
    b. Nixon.
    c. Eisenhower.
    d. Carter.

9. George W. Bush's appointment of which cabinet official caused controversy in 2001?
   a. Colin Powell.
   b. John Ashcroft.
   c. Condoleeza Rice.
   d. Donald Rumsfeld.

10. Which of the following is usually ranked as one of the "ten best" presidents?
    a. Nixon.
    b. Coolidge.
    c. Eisenhower.
    d. Grant.

Part V — Test Answers

Pretest

1.	b	6.	c
2.	c	7.	b
3.	a	8.	c
4.	a	9.	b
5.	a	10.	c

Programmed Review

1.	admired, feared	20.	did
2.	leadership	21.	recruitment
3.	character; integrity	22.	Hillary
4.	dictators	23.	OMB
5.	limited	24.	followers
6.	checks and balances	25.	Cheney
7.	natural-born	26.	press conference
8.	parliamentary	27.	opinion polls
9.	civilian	28.	more
10.	conflict, interest	29.	staff
11.	New Deal	30.	Management, Budget
12.	Senate	31.	Cabinet
13.	coalition	32.	Twenty-Fifth
14.	Union	33.	parliamentary
15.	line,staff	34.	adversary
16.	television	35.	more
17.	public's	36.	Rich
18.	party	37.	Truman
19.	chief	38.	Harding

Post Test

1.	a	6.	c
2.	a	7.	b
3.	b	8.	a

4. d
5. b

9. b
10. a

Chapter 13
Congress and the President

PART I—GUIDEPOSTS

1. Introduction to Congressional-Presidential Relations
   a. How would one characterize the history of congressional-presidential relationships?
   b. What challenges must a new president face regarding dealings with Congress?
   c. What are the key factors that will determine whether a president succeeds or fails in his dealings with Congress?

2. Separate but Equal Branches
   a. Why did the framers see Congress as the central or main branch of government?
   b. How can Congress still impose its will upon the president?
   c. Despite the potential for conflict, how can the two branches still cooperate?

3. Sources of Discord
   a. Why does Congress often see things differently than the president?
   b. What is the impact of office terms, different constituencies, parties, public support, divided government, and the need for supermajorities upon the congressional-presidential relationship?

4. The Ebb and Flow of Power Between the Branches
   a. How/why have members of Congress and the president clashed over war powers?
   b. How do controversies over confirmation politics affect the presidential-congressional relationship?
   c. What is the significance of executive orders, executive privilege, the veto, impoundment, and continuing resolutions?
   d. Why do the two branches frequently clash over the federal budget?
   e. What political lessons can be discerned from the Clinton impeachment process?

5. Building Coalitions/The President's Agenda
   a. How does public support help the president with Congress?
   b. How can the president win friends and influence in Congress?
   c. In what ways can Congress set/shape the national policy agenda?
   d. Why was partisanship set aside after the 9/11 attacks?
   e. What are the two kinds of resources that shape a presidential agenda?
   f. What is meant by a "mandate" to govern?
   g. What is the "cycle of decreasing influence" and the "cycle of increasing effectiveness"?

PART II—PRETEST

1. A president formally proposes his legislative agenda through
   - a. the State of the Union Address.
   - b. his rationales for vetoes.
   - c. his cabinet.
   - d. all of the above.

2. Each term of a House member is
   - a. six years.
   - b. four years.
   - c. five years.
   - d. none of the above.

3. A president who had only one term in office would have served
   - a. three years.
   - b. four years.
   - c. two years.
   - d. eight years.

4. "Divided government" means that
   - a. the president is not getting along with his cabinet.
   - b. Congress has few policy proposals to offer vs. the president's agenda.
   - c. one party does not control both the presidency and the two houses of Congress.
   - d. all of the above

5. A presidential directive that has the force of law is called
   - a. impoundment.
   - b. executive privilege.
   - c. an executive order.
   - d. an executive veto.

6. The president who first gave executive privilege a bad name was
   - a. Gerald Ford.
   - b. Richard Nixon.
   - c. Bill Clinton.
   - d. Jimmy Carter.

7. A method by which the president can win friends and influence in Congress is through
   - a. campaign assistance.
   - b. patronage.
   - c. bill signing ceremonies.
   - d. all of the above.

8. Some political experts would like the U.S. to adopt a
   - a. parliamentary system.
   - b. unitary system.
   - c. confederation system.
   - c. non-democratic political system.

9. The type of veto declared unconstitutional by the Supreme Court in 1998 was the
   - a. pocket veto.
   - b. unitary system
   - c. item veto.
   - d. none of the above

10. The War Powers Act was passed in the aftermath of the
   - a. second World War.
   - c. Korean War.

b. first World War.   d.   Vietnam War.

PART III—PROGRAMMED REVIEW

Knowledge Objective: To understand the basic ideas underlying congressional-presidential relations
  1. President George W. Bush came to office without a national _____.
  2. A major congressional rival confronting President Bush was Senator John _____.
  3. The framers saw separation of powers as a political (strength or weakness) _____ the Constitution.
  4. Congress and President George W. Bush seemed to set aside partisan differences after the terrorist attacks of _____.

Knowledge Objective: To understand the political importance of "separate but equal branches"
  5. The Constitution's writers saw the _____ branch as dominant.
  6. Civil war president _____ gained additional presidential powers.
  7. Congress can impose its will, as witnessed by President _____'s problems with health care.
  8. Congress jealously guards its policy preferences in the fields of _____ and _____.

Knowledge Objective: To understand why Congress has a different political perspective
  9. Presidents have implied, inherent, or _____ powers.
  10. The president, unlike Congress, has a _____ perspective.
  11. Senators serve for _____ year terms.
  12. Most members of Congress run their campaigns _____ of party.
  13. The most important predictor of how members of Congress vote is _____ affiliation.
  14. _____ votes are needed to end a filibuster.

Knowledge Objective: To understand why there is controversy between the branches
  15. The president (has, does not have) the power to declare war.
  16. Some scholars argue that Congress has been ____ and abdicated its authority to the president.
  17. The War Powers Resolution was passed over President _____'s veto.
  18. The Senate has rejected _____ proposed cabinet members.
  19. George W. Bush nominated _____ as his attorney general. He was a controversial choice.
  20. Executive privilege was used by Clinton vis-à-vis his foreign policy stance toward _____.
  21. An executive order has the force of _____.
  22. Congress has overridden less than _____ percent of presidents' regular vetoes.
  23. President Nixon practiced _____, not spending funds for purposes Congress had authorized.
  24. President Clinton was impeached by the _____, but not convicted by the _____.

74

25. The Budget Act of _____ tried to restore greater budget making to Congress.

Knowledge Objective: To understand the importance of coalition-building and the president's agenda
26. _____ support is crucial to a president's success with Congress.
27. Appointing the friends and political supporters of key members of Congress to various federal positions is called _____.
28. Kennedy, Reagan, and Clinton were considered _____ (effective, ineffective) communicators.
29. The "genius" of Congress is deliberation, debate, and _____.
30. The two types of resources that shape a president's agenda are _____ and _____-_____.

PART IV—POST-TEST

1. The Secretary of Defense nominee rejected by the Senate in 1989 was
   a. Lewis L. Strauss.
   b. Charles B. Warren.
   c.　John Tower.
   d.　none of these.

2. According to the War Powers Resolution, Congress can end a future troop commitment within
   a. 60 days.
   b. 30 days.
   c.　90 days.
   d.　120 days.

3. The type of veto that is associated with the period of "ten days" is termed the
   a. item veto.
   b. regular veto.
   c.　pocket veto.
   d.　all of the above

4. The U.S. president who issued the greatest number of regular vetoes was
   a. Richard Nixon.
   b. John F. Kennedy.
   c.　George Bush.
   d.　Franklin D. Roosevelt.

5. The president who used executive orders more than 350 times was
   a. Ronald Reagan.
   b. Bill Clinton.
   c.　Jimmy Carter.
   d.　Lyndon Johnson

6. Senate Democrats defeated which Bush nominee for the Fifth Circuit Court of Appeals in 2002?
   a. Clarence Thomas
   b. Charles Pickering
   c.　John Ashcroft
   d.　Linda Chavez

7. All of the following are "supermajorities" EXCEPT
   a. 60 votes to end a filibuster.
   b. two-thirds vote to override a presidential veto.
   c. a majority - 51 votes - needed to pass a bill in the Senate.
   d. None of the above is a supermajority.

8. Compared to the president, Congress, in a national crisis, is
   a. slower to act.
   b. faster to act.
   c. unable to respond at all in any way.
   d. slower, but always wiser.

9. Of the presidents Eisenhower to Clinton, which president achieved the lowest congressional support percentage in the early 1990s?
   a. George Bush
   b. Bill Clinton
   c. Ronald Reagan
   d. Jimmy Carter

10. Which of the following congressional qualities conspires against presidential policy leadership?
    a. Its institutional responsibilities and pride
    b. Its decentralized nature
    c. Its independent and entrepreneurial mode of legislators
    d. all of the above

PART V—TEST ANSWERS

Pretest

1. a
2. d
3. b
4. c
5. c
6. b
7. d
8. a
9. b
10. d

Post-test

1. c
2. a
3. c
4. d
5. b
6. b
7. c
8. a
9. a
10. d

Programmed Review

1. mandate
2. McCain
3. strength
4. 9/11
5. Congressional
6. Lincoln
7. Clinton
8. defense/agriculture
9. emergency
10. national
16. passive
17. Nixon
18. nine
19. Ashcroft
20. Haiti
21. law
22. ten
23. impoundment
24. House, Senate
25. 1974

11. six
12. independently
13. partisan
14. Sixty
15. does not have

26. Public
27. patronage
28. effective
29. reflection
30. Political; decision-making

Chapter 14
The Bureaucracy: The Real Power?

PART I — GUIDEPOSTS

1. Federal Government is Big
   a. What is the employment level of federal government?
   b. What are the chief characteristics of the bureaucracy?
   c. What is the public's attitudes toward government?

2. Overview of the Federal Bureaucracy
   a. What is a bureaucratic organization?
   b. What do bureaucrats do?
   c. Why is the bureaucracy an inviting target for critics?
   d. What are the basic facts about the size, location, and jobs in the bureaucracy?
   e. Describe the formal way in which the federal bureaucracy is organized.
   f. How does the informal organization differ?
   g. How did the bureaucracy evolve?

3. The United States Civil Service
   a. Why was the original spoils system replaced by a merit system?
   b. What was the objective of the Hatch Act? How has it been revised?

4. Bureaucracy in Action
   a. On what assumptions is the textbook model of organization based?
   b. What are some limitations placed upon the textbook model?
   c. What are the essential points about the bureaucracy as illustrated by the career of George Brown?
   d. Why do bureaucracies tend to expand in size?

5. Public View of the Bureaucracy
   a. Why is there widespread public hostility toward bureaucrats?
   b. Do the common complaints about bureaucracy have a factual base?
   c. Why do we have red tape in our system?
   d. Do government agencies ever fade away?
   e. How does the existing U.S. bureaucracy compare with that of other major nations?
   f. How has "sunshine legislation" helped?

6. Bureaucratic Responsiveness and Accountability
   a. On the broad scene, is our bureaucracy responsive to citizen needs?
   b. What is privatization, who are the supporters, who are the critics?
   c. What leverage do presidents have in controlling bureaucrats?
   d. Why is the OMB such a major force?
   e. What form does bureaucratic resistance to change take?
   f. How does Congress exert control over bureaucrats?
   g. What is the major reason that congressional oversight is often weak?
   h. Why do we lack a simple answer to the questions of bureaucratic reform and control?

PART II — PRETEST

1. Depending on the observer, red tape can be described in *all but one* of the following ways.
    a. an inevitability of government
    b. civil service employees who serve under the merit system
    c. rigid procedures
    d. a bureaucracy that is more interested in means than ends

2. Nearly twenty-five percent of all civilian employees of the federal government work for
    a. defense agencies.
    b. the Social Security Administration.
    c. welfare agencies.
    d. the Interstate Commerce Commission.

3. Most independent agencies of government are created by
    a. the president.
    b. Congress
    c. the cabinet.
    d. none of the above.

4. An example of a government corporation is
    a. Securities and Exchange Commission.
    b. U.S. Mint.
    c. Government Printing Office.
    d. FDIC.

5. Independent regulatory boards have *all but one* of these special characteristics.
    a. They do not report directly to the president.
    b. They perform legislative functions.
    c. Their members are political appointees whose terms coincide with the president's.
    d. They have judicial functions.

6. A landmark law creating a merit system of civil service was the congressional act named for its sponsor.
    a. Garfield
    b. Sedman
    c.
    c. Pendleton
    d. Hatch

7. The OPM plays *all but one* of the following roles in recruiting new civil service employees.
    a. administers and scores tests
    b. designates the individual an agency must hire
    c. creates a ranked register of successful applicants
    d. certifies three names for each agency vacancy

8. The Hatch Act provides that government employees can do all except
    a. make campaign contributions.
    b. attend political rallies.
    c. assist in voter registration.
    d. sell political fund-raising tickets to subordinates.

9. The General Services Administration best exemplifies a(an):
    a. independent agency.
    b. independent regulatory board.
    c. government corporation.
    d. bureau.

10. The weakest relationship of most federal administrators is with
    a. fellow colleagues.
    b. lobbyists.
    c. congressional committees.
    d. the president.

PART III — PROGRAMMED REVIEW

Knowledge Objective: To examine the shape of federal bureaucracy
1. The bureaucracy consists of _____ cabinet-level departments.
2. Nearly _____ percent of all federal civilian employees work for the defense agencies.
3. Bureaucracy originally referred to a _____, _____ method of organization.
4. Most federal employees are _____ collar workers.
5. The federal level of bureaucracy has (grown, decreased) _____ in the past few years.
6. Federal employees are _____ representative of the nation as a whole than legislators.
7. The common basis for organization of a department is _____ .
8. An example of a government _____ is the Corporation for Public Broadcasting.
9. A weak link in the bureaucracy are the _____ secretaries.

Knowledge Objective: To trace the evolution of the U.S. Civil Service
10. The _____ system permitted newly elected presidents to appoint their supporters.
11. Restrictions on the political activities of federal employees were imposed by the _____ Act.
12. Federal employees (may, may not) _____ take an active part in partisan politics.
13. The IRS only audits _____ people a year.
14. After a bill becomes law, bureaucrats must be concerned with the law being _____.

Knowledge Objective: To analyze the public's view of bureaucracy
15. Most Americans support bureaucracy that operates in their interest while being critical of big bureaucracy in the _____ .
16. Critics contend a central problem with bureaucracy is our failure to _____ and _____ it.
17. About _____ of federal employees have joined unions.
18. The _____ of a federal agency is the _____ rather than the rule.
19. An _____ agency is not tied to any of the three branches.
20. The complex rules and regulations under which bureaucracy functions is called _____ _____.
21. The process of contracting out public services to private organizations is called _____ .

Knowledge Objective: To discover the controls under which bureaucrats operate
22. Major control of bureaucracy is shared by _____ and the _____ .
23. The Civil Service Reform Act (1978) created a top grade of career bureaucrats, the _____ _____ _____ .
24. Supporters of the patronage system believe that the existing _____ system of federal employment encourages deadwood.
25. _____ is the executive office responsible for managing the federal bureaucracy.
26. The responsiveness of bureaucrats is limited by the procedures that make them _____ .

PART IV — POST-TEST

1. The largest subunit of a government department is usually called a
    a. bureau.
    b. division.
    c. commission.
    d. cabin.

2. Presidents like to reorganize the bureaucracy because
    a. managerial controls can be increased.
    b. priorities can be symbolized.
    c. policy integration can be improved.
    d. all of the above.

3. Congress normally controls the bureaucracy in all of the following ways except
    a. budgetary appropriation.
    b. holding hearings.
    c. confirmation of personnel.
    d. firing civil servants.

4. How many federal jobs were eliminated by the Clinton-Gore administration?
    a. 200,000
    b. 300,000
    c. 500,000
    d. 600,000

5. An example of informal organization would be when a superior and his subordinates
    a. hunt and fish together.
    b. confer over bureau policy.
    c. jointly evaluate employees for promotion.
    d. establish long-range budget plans.

6. Who controls the bureaucracy?
    a. the president
    d. Congress
    e. no single power
    d. the voter

7. In practice the Senior Executive Service has
    a. been successful.
    b. been a failure.
    c. had little impact.
    d. transformed the Civil Service.

8. An effective device for implementing the president's wishes is the
    a. Senior Executive Service.
    b. Office of Management and Budget.
    c. Civil Service Reform Act.
    d. Assistant Secretaries.

9. The responsiveness of a bureaucracy is closely linked to its
    a. accountability.
    b. security.

c. clientele.
d. computer capability.

10. Privatization is:
    a. the commissioning of merchant ships as a part of the navy.
    b. secrecy of interoffice memos.
    c. president's right to withhold his IRS return.
    d. placing certain government functions in the private sector.

PART V — TEST ANSWERS

Pretest

1. b	6. c
2. a	7. b
3. b	8. d
4. d	9. a
5. c	10. d

Programmed Review

1. fourteen	15. abstract
2. twenty-five	16. control; discipline
3. rational, efficient	17. one-third
4. white	18. death; exception
5. decreased	19. independent
6. more	20. red tape
7. function	21. fourteen
8. corporation	22. privatization
9. assistant	23. Congress; President
10. spoils	24. Senior Executive Service
11. Hatch	25. tenure
12. may not	26. OMB
13. 2 million	27. accountable
14. implemented	

Post-test

1. a	6. c
2. d	7. c
3. d	8. b
4. b	9. a
5. a	10. d

Chapter 15
The Judiciary: The Balancing Branch

PART I — GUIDEPOSTS

1. The Scope of Judicial Power
   a. How did the first judges of the Supreme Court shape its authority and scope?
   b. Why is our system called adversarial?
   c. What kinds of disputes do they hear? What are justiciable disputes?
   d. Why have class action suits become so important?
   e. Define plaintiff, defendant, plea bargain, public defender, and judicial review.
   f. What is the relationship between state and federal courts in the U.S.?

2. The Federal Judicial System
   a. By what body was the federal court system established?
   b. What courts form the base of the federal judicial system? What do they do?
   c. What cases reach the Courts of Appeal? How do they relate to state courts?
   d. What other types of federal courts exist?

3. The Politics of Appointing Federal Judges
   a. What groups have an input in the selection process?
   b. Why is the Senate Judiciary Committee so important? What is senatorial courtesy?
   c. How much attention is paid to party, race, and gender in nominating judges?
   d. How important is ideology?
   e. Why is age such a vital factor?
   f. What role does ideology play? When applied to the Court, what is the meaning of judicial activism and self-restraint?
   g. How did the nomination hearings of Bork, Souter, Thomas, Breyer, and Ginsburg differ? Also, why is Justice Sandra Day O'Connor important to the Court's future?
   h. Is change likely for the selection process of judges?
   i. What authority does Congress have over jurisdiction and membership of the Court?
   j. Do judges make law? What are the "types of laws"?
   k. What is *stare decisis*? How does it affect what the judges decide?

4. The Supreme Court and How It Operates
   a. What devices give the Court an air of authority and respect?
   b. How does the Supreme Court decide what cases it will hear?
   c. What is the "rule of four"? Also, why has the Court's caseload increased?
   d. What procedure is used by the Court in hearing cases? What is *amicus curiae*?
   e. Why are Court conferences so important?
   f. Who writes the Court opinion? What if the vote is split?
   g. Why is such an effort put into consensus voting?
   h. How have the styles of recent chief justices varied?
   i. Why is the implementation of many Court decisions long delayed?
   j. What are the roles of the law clerks and the Solicitor General?

5. Judicial Power in a Constitutional Democracy

a. Does our system of justice put power in the hands of unelected officials?

b. Does public opinion have any impact?

c. Who favors judicial activism? Judicial restraint? Are conservatives and liberals apt to change roles in this argument? Why?

d. What can Congress do if it disagrees with a Court decision?

PART II — PRETEST

1. Procedure in the Supreme Court is surrounded by considerable ceremony. *All but one* of the following procedures is customary.
   a. The justices are always attired in their robes of office.
   b. Government attorneys wear morning clothes.
   c. All judges are seated in alphabetical order.
   d. Judges are introduced by the Clerk of the Court.

2. The chief basis for judicial decisions is probably
   a. precedent.
   b. public opinion.
   c. the party in power.
   d. checks and balances.

3. The judicial doctrine of *stare decisis* provides that the courts decide cases largely on the basis of
   a. present economic and social conditions.
   b. earlier court decisions.
   c. interpreting the will of Congress.
   d. equity.

4. Federal courts of appeal normally have
   a. original jurisdiction.
   b. grand juries.
   c. three-judge jury.
   d. judges with ten-year terms.

5. No decision can be rendered by the Supreme Court unless
   a. all nine judges participate.
   b. a quorum of five is present.
   c. six judges participate.
   d. at least two judges represent majority opinion.

6. At the Friday conference of Supreme Court justices, *all but one* of the following is true.
   a. The chief justice presides.
   b. The chief justice votes first.
   c. Each justice carries a red leather book.
   d. A majority decides the case.

7. The powers of the chief justice include *all but one* of the following.
   a. presiding over the Court
   b. choosing the opinion writer if justice has voted with the majority
   c. barring dissenting justices from the Friday conference
   d. leading conference discussion

8. The "rule of four" in Supreme Court procedure provides that four judges
    a. may adjourn the Court.
    b. grant a writ of certiorari.
    c. give priority to the order of hearing a case.
    d. are a quorum.

9. Critics of judicial activism believe that the courts should not try to make policy because
    a. judges are not elected.
    b. they do not represent all regions of the country.
    c. their terms do not coincide with that of the president.
    d. they do not have the necessary expertise.

10. After a grueling hearing that outraged women and liberal groups, the Senate Judiciary Committee narrowly confirmed
    a. Antonin Scalia.
    b. David Souter.
    c. Clarence Thomas.
    d. Sandra O'Connor.

PART III — PROGRAMMED PREVIEW

Knowledge Objective: **To describe the differing forms of law on which the American legal system is based**
1. Law based on judicial decisions of medieval English judges is _____ law.
2. Law based on judicial interpretation of the Constitution is _____ law.
3. A specific act of legislative body is _____ law.
4. Law based on exceptions from the common law in the interests of justice is _____ law.
5. The code of law emerging from bureaucratic decisions is _____ law.
6. The rule of precedent under which federal courts operate is called _____ _____.
7. The concept that the courts should serve as a neutral referee between two contending parties is called the _____ system.

Knowledge Objective: **To gain an overview of the organization of the federal court system**
8. The lowest federal courts, in which nearly 700 judges preside, are _____ courts.
9. The federal courts that review district court decisions are courts of _____.
10. The highest federal court, with both original and appellate jurisdiction, is the _____ _____.
11. The right to review cases already considered is _____ _____.
12. The top U.S. prosecutor is the _____ _____.
13. State and federal courts (do, do not) _____ exist in a superior-inferior relationship.
14. Much of the lower judicial work of the U.S. district is now carried out by _____.
15. Decisions of regulatory agencies can be reviewed by courts of _____.
16. Persons charged with a crime may get a reduced sentence by agreeing to a(n) _____ _____.
17. The court officer who determines most appeals heard by the Supreme Court is the _____ _____.

Knowledge Objective: **To study the major participants involved in selection of federal judges**

18. The custom that requires the president to consult with a state's senators before nominating a federal judge is called _____ _____.
19. All potential nominees for federal judgeships are_____ by the American Bar Association.
20. In naming federal judges, the political affiliation of the nominee may be less important than the person's _____.
21. Presidential nominations to the Supreme Court are reviewed by the Senate _____ _____.
22. In an attempt to avoid another Bork nomination battle, Bush nominated Souter, who had no _____ past record.
23. Bush's most controversial nomination to the Supreme Court was _____.
24. Congress controls the _____ and _____ of federal courts.

Knowledge Objective: **To discover how the Supreme Court operates**
25. The only cases heard by the Supreme Court are those selected by the _____ _____.
26. Cases previously decided by lower courts are called up to the Supreme Court by writs of _____.
27. The normal upper time limit granted to counsel for each side in arguing a Supreme Court case is _____ _____.
28. Supreme Court decisions are made in secret each week at the _____ _____.
29. One use of published Supreme Court _____ is to communicate with the general public.

Knowledge Objective: **To evaluate the role of judicial review in a democratic society**
30. Over the past forty years more than 1,000 acts of _____ and _____ _____ have been invalidated by the Supreme Court.
31. When the Supreme Court becomes greatly involved in political life, it is known as an _____ court.
32. Critics who believe that the Supreme Court has become too activist charge it with engaging in _____ _____.
33. Chief Justice Rehnquist believes judges do pay attention to the great tides of _____ _____.
34. The opponents of judicial activism believe that the Court should not become involved in _____ making.

PART IV — POST-TEST

1. An activist court, the critics say, is overly zealous in protecting the
   a. poor.
   b. property owners.
   c. state officials.
   d. military officers.

2. The federal court that has only original jurisdiction is
   a. the Supreme Court.
   b. district courts.
   c. courts of appeal.
   d. lower courts.

3. An adversary system of justice is one in which
   a. the police bring charges.
   b. the court is a neutral referee.
   c. judges are political appointees.
   d. justice is based on majority vote.

86

4. The top national official who has openly favored minority considerations in the judicial selection process has been
   a. Carter.
   b. Burger.
   c. Ford.
   d. Reagan.

5. The law that evolved from decisions interpreting our basic national governing document is
   a. constitutional law.
   b. administrative law.
   c. equity law.
   d. statutory law.

6. Several justices have timed their retirement to
   a. ensure a replacement by a president sharing their views.
   b. increase their retirement benefits.
   c. bring fresh ideas to the Court.
   d. avoid ruling on an issue where they have no competence.

7. Elections eventually influence Supreme Court decisions because
   a. the judges try to do what the people want.
   b. judges who are out of step are impeached.
   c. new judges are appointed.
   d. interest groups influence decisions.

8. In federal courts, justifiable disputes are
   a. all constitutional questions.
   b. those involving actual cases.
   c. all administrative decisions.
   d. those involving political questions.

9. The relationship between the state and federal court systems is
   a. federal courts are always superior.
   b. state courts have original jurisdiction.
   c. they have interrelated responsibility.
   d. they are completely separate.

10. If a Supreme Court justice agrees with the majority decision but differs on the reasoning, he files
    a. a concurring opinion.
    b. a dissenting opinion.
    c. articles of agreement.
    d. a minority opinion.

PART V — TEST ANSWERS

Pretest

1. c	6. b
2. a	7. c
3. b	8. b
4. c	9. a
5. c	10. c

Programmed Review

1. common
2. constitutional
3. statutory
4. equity
5. administrative
6. *stare decisis*
7. adversary
8. district
9. appeal
10. Supreme Court
11. Appellate jurisdiction
12. Attorney General
13. do not
14. magistrates
15. appeal
16. plea bargain
17. solicitor general
18. senatorial courtesy
19. evaluated
20. ideology
21. Judiciary Committee
22. visible
23. Thomas
24. structure; jurisdiction
25. Supreme Court
26. certiorari
27. thirty minutes
28. Friday conference
29. opinion
30. legislatures; city councils
31. activist
32. Judicial legislation
33. public opinion
34. policy

Post-test

1. a
2. b
3. b
4. a
5. a
6. a
7. c
8. b
9. c
10. a

Chapter 16
First Amendment Freedoms

PART I — GUIDEPOSTS

1. Rights in the Original Constitution/The Bill of Rights and the States
    a. What rights are guaranteed to U.S. citizens by the First Amendment?
    b. To what level of government did the Bill of Rights originally apply?
    c. What are the two reasons why a Bill of Rights was added to the U.S. Constitution?
    d. What was the impact of *Gitlow v. New York*?
    e. Today, what trend has developed at the state level to enlarge the federal Bill of Rights?
    f. What is habeas corpus, an ex post facto law, and a bill of attainder?
    g. How have the Bill of Rights been applied to the states?

2. Freedom of Religion
    a. What is meant by an "establishment of religion"? Why did our colonial experience prompt this prohibition?
    b. Why did Congress enact the Religious Freedom Restoration Act of 1993?
    c. How does the "free exercise" clause affect the right to freedom of worship?

3. Free Speech and Free People
    a. Why did Justice Holmes believe that free speech was the best test of truth?
    b. How does the Constitution distinguish speech, belief, and action?
    c. Indicate the differences between protected and unprotected speech under the:
        •   bad tendency test
        •   clear present and danger test
        •   preferred position doctrine
    d. Why is freedom of speech fundamentally important to democracy?
    e. Why is the Supreme Court skeptical of all forms of prior restraint?
    f. Why does the Supreme Court challenge restrictions on speech that it regards as vague or overly broad?

4. Non-protected and Protected Speech
    a. What is libel? Why are public and private persons treated differently under libel laws? What is the significance of the *New York Times v. Sullivan?*
    b. How much authority do local communities have in declaring materials obscene?
    c. What groups have formed a coalition to oppose pornography?
    d. How has the Canadian Supreme Court redefined obscenity?
    e. What events prompted the Sedition Act of 1798?
    f. Why is commercial speech subject to greater regulation than other forms of speech?

5.	Freedom of the Press/Other Media and Communications
	a.	What is the definition of press?
	b.	What special rights does the press believe it has? Why? Has the Supreme Court agreed?
	c.	What is a sunshine law? What effect does it have on governmental operations?
	d.	What has been the impact of the Freedom of Information Act?
	e.	What was the Supreme Court ruling in the NEA grant case?
	f.	Does TV coverage prevent a fair trial? Why or why not?
	g.	Are special restrictions applied to the mails, motion pictures, handbills, sound tracks, billboards, and advertising?
	h.	What developments during recent years have thrown the special status of TV broadcasters into question?
	i.	What constitutional problems are created by cable television communications?
	j	What special issues are posed by Internet communications? How does the Communications Decency and Telecommunications Act affect cyberspace?
	k.	What are the constitutional questions regarding the Communications Decency Act of 1996? What was the gist of *Reno v. ACLU*? Also, what was "COPA"?

6.	Freedom of Assembly
	a.	Cite several "assemblies" that led to concern for public order. What sort of statutes are necessary to deal with such issues?
	b.	How does the place that a rally is held have a bearing on its legality?
	c.	What was significant about the "Million Youth March" in New York City?
	d.	What is the significance of civil disobedience?
	e.	What is the constitutional test for injunctions on abortion clinic protests?

PART II — PRETEST

1.	Specifically, the Bill of Rights ratified in 1791 was aimed at
	a.	the national government.
	b.	the state governments.
	c.	both national and state government.
	d.	providing unlimited freedom to the people.

2.	The due process clause, interpreted to mean that the states could not abridge the First Amendment freedoms, is part of the
	a.	Fifteenth Amendment.	c.	Eighteenth Amendment.
	b.	Fourteenth Amendment.	d.	Thirteenth Amendment.

3. Because of the Establishment Clause, states may not
    a. teach the Darwinian theory of evolution.
    b. study the Bible or religion in public schools.
    c. permit religious instructors to teach in public schools during the day.
    d. establish Blue Laws.

4. The Supreme Court has held that tax funds may not be used to
    a. provide sign-language interpretation for deaf parochial school students.
    b. furnish guidance and remedial help in parochial schools.
    c. pay fares to send children to church-operated schools.
    d. pay parochial teachers' salaries.

5. The doctrine that free speech cannot be restricted unless there is a close connection between a speech and illegal action is called
    a. the clear and present danger test.
    b. the speech and dangerous result test.
    c. the speech and action test.
    d absolutist doctrine.

6. Of all forms of government interference with expression, judges are most suspicious of those that
    a. trespass on First Amendment freedoms.
    b. limit freedom of speech of any kind.
    c. impose prior restraints on publication.
    d. impose *a posteriori* restraints.

7. The current standards for obscenity are made
    a. by the Supreme Court.   c. at the community level.
    b. at the state level.   d. by Congress.

8. Persons may be convicted for one of the following.
    a. possessing obscene materials
    b. selling obscene literature
    c. importing obscene literature from abroad
    d. writing obscene material

9. Street marches by protest groups are protected by the First Amendment right to
    a. assemble.   c. demonstrate.
    b. petition.   d. boycott.

10. All of the following are forms of non-protected speech except
    a. libel.   c. obscenity.
    b. symbolic speech.   d. commercial speech.

PART III — PROGRAMMED REVIEW

Knowledge Objective: To examine constitutional safeguards of freedom
1. The first ten amendments to the Constitution are known as _____.
2. The nationalization of the Bill of Rights was an _____ process whereby the Supreme Court selectively applied them to state and local governments via the due process clause.
3. The _____ _____ clause of the Fourteenth Amendment protects freedom of the press and of speech from impairment by the states.
4. *Gitlow v. New York* (1925) extended the _____ amendment rights via the Fourteenth Amendment.

Knowledge Objective: To inquire into the meaning of the wall of separation between church and state
5. The _____ clause is designed to prevent three main evils: sponsorship, financial support, and active involvement of the government in religious activity.
6. The _____ restored use of the compelling interest test.
7. The Supreme Court has held that a publicly sponsored Nativity scene (is, is not) _____ constitutional if the basic purpose is commercial.
8. Because of the Establishment Clause, states may not prohibit the teaching of Darwin's theory of evolution or require the simultaneous teaching of

   _____ _____.
9. The Supreme Court has ruled that tax funds (may, may not) _____ be used for lunches, transportation, and remedial assistance in religious primary and secondary schools.
10. Sponsorship of prayer in school buildings by public school authorities (is, is not) _____ constitutional.
11. The Supreme Court (has, has not) _____ upheld the right of parents to deduct from their state taxes expenses incurred in sending children to public or private schools.

Knowledge Objective: To analyze the relationship between free speech and a free people
12. Government's constitutional power to regulate speech involves three forms: beliefs, speech, and _____.
13. The limits of free speech were set forth as the _____ _____ _____ _____ test by Justice Holmes in *Schenck v. United States*.
14. The _____ position doctrine takes the view that freedom of expression has the highest priority.
15. Of all forms of governmental interference with expression, judges are most suspicious of those that impose _____ restraint on publication.
16. When people of common intelligence differ on the requirements of a law, it is unconstitutional on the grounds of _____.

Knowledge Objective: To investigate the scope of freedom of the press

17. In a recent decision the Supreme Court (did, did not) _____ support barring of the press from a criminal case.

18. In 1996, Congress made it a federal crime to use the _____ to knowingly transmit indecent material to minors.

19. More than ____ percent of requests under the FOIA have been granted.

20. Censorship of the mails is _____.

21. The _____ _____ _____ acts make most nonclassified records of federal agencies public.

22. Many states have passed_____ laws requiring most government agencies to open their meetings to the public and the press.

23. Household censorship is (constitutional, unconstitutional)_____.

24. The federal regulation of radio and television is based on the _____ of broadcast channels available.

25. Current federal laws (do/do not)_____ protect commercial speech.

Knowledge Objective: To define limits on speech (libel, obscenity) that are constitutional

26. The First Amendment (does, does not) _____ prevent the FCC from refusing to renew a radio license if in its opinion a broadcaster has not served the public interest.

27. The _____ _____ doctrine concerns censorship before a speech is made.

28. The mere fact that a statement is wrong or even defamatory is not sufficient to sustain a charge of _____.

29. Under the current test a jury determines whether or not a work appeals to prurient interests or is patently offensive to _____ standards.

30. Obscenity (is, is not) _____ entitled to constitutional protection.

31. Pornographic books and x-rated movies are entitled to (less, the same) _____ protection than political speech.

32. Cities may regulate by _____ where adult motion picture theaters may be located.

33. Sexually explicit materials either about minors or aimed at them (are/are not) _____ prohibited by the First Amendment.

Knowledge Objective: To examine the right of the people peaceably to assemble and to petition the government

34. The right to assemble peaceably applies not only to meetings in private homes, but to gatherings held in _____ _____.

35. The right to assemble and to petition does not include the right to _____ on private property.

36. The right of the Million Youth Rally to march on the streets (has, has not) _____ been upheld by the courts.

37. In the late eighteenth century the _____ Act made it a crime to utter false, scandalous, or malicious statements intended to bring the government or any of its officers into disrepute.

38. In general, peaceful civil disobedience (is/is not) _____ a protected right.
39. Seditious speech (is/is not) _____ protected when it advocates violence.
40. Privately owned shopping malls are neither public _____ nor places of public _____.

PART IV — POST-TEST

1. What types of governmental meetings are not open to the public?
   a. judicial conferences
   b. federal trials
   c. congressional committee meetings
   d. local school board meetings

2. The bad tendency doctrine gives to _____ the power to decide what kinds of speech can be outlawed.
   a. courts
   b. legislatures
   c. the people
   d. chief executives

3. Constitutional restrictions on establishment of religion include
   a. persons praying in school buildings.
   b. classes observing a moment of silence.
   c. public officials sponsoring nondenominational prayer at primary and secondary school graduations.
   d. studying the Bible.

4. The Freedom of Information Act of 1966 concerns
   a. censorship.
   b. press responsibility and fairness.
   c. abuses in the over classification of documents.
   d. the right to privacy.

5. The Telecommunications Act of 1996 provided for all but one of the following.
   a. competition among telephone companies and cable TV
   b. requirement of v-chips in new television sets
   c. elimination of government regulation of the airways
   d. Communications Decency Act

6. In *Miller v. California* (1973), Chief Justice Burger defined obscenity as a work that
   a. lacks serious artistic, political, or scientific value.
   b. does not apply traditional standards of morality.
   c. is utterly without redeeming value.
   d. graphically describes sexual activity.

7. The distribution of religious and political pamphlets, leaflets, and handbills to the public is
    a. constitutionally protected.
    b. under almost all circumstances locally prosecuted.
    c. constitutionally ignored.
    d. prohibited without a license.

8. Of the following, which has the greatest restrictions placed upon it by the Constitution?
    a. speech
    b. assembly
    c. picketing
    d. petitions

9. Persons may have no constitutional right to engage in political action in
    a. any area designed to serve purposes other than demonstrations.
    b. courthouses.
    c. schools.
    d. privately owned shopping malls.

10. "Shield laws" pertain to freedom of
    a. assembly.
    b. the press.
    c. motion picture producers.
    d. Internet use.

PART V — TEST ANSWERS

Pretest

1.	a		6.	c
2.	b		7.	c
3.	c		8.	c
4.	d		9.	a
5.	a		10.	b

Programmed Review

1.	Bill of Rights	20.	unconstitutional.
2.	evolutionary	21.	Freedom of Information
3.	due process	22.	sunshine
4.	First	23.	constitutional
5.	Establishment	24.	scarcity
6.	The Restoration of Religious Freedom Act of 1993	25.	do not
		26.	does not
7.	is	27.	prior restraint
8.	creation science	28.	libel
9.	may	29.	community

10. is not
11. has
12. action
13. clear and present danger
14. preferred
15. prior
16. vagueness
17. did not
18. Internet
19. ninety

30. is not
31. less
32. zoning
33. are
34. public streets
35. trespass
36. has
37. Sedition
38. is not
39. is not
40. streets, assembly

Post-test

1. a
2. b
3. c
4. c
5. c

6. a
7. a
8. c
9. d
10. b

Chapter 17
Rights to Life, Liberty, Property

PART I — GUIDEPOSTS

1. Introduction/Citizenship Rights
   a. How does our government compare to others?
   b. What is due process?
   c. How did the 2001 terrorist attacks create the liberty-security issue?
   d. How are the rights/liberties of individuals affected during wartime?

2. The Constitution Protects Citizenship
   a. Explain the relationship between a child's citizenship and his/her parents.
   b. In what ways did the Fourteenth Amendment give constitutional protection to citizenship?
   c. What are the steps in naturalization?
   d. What are some of the privileges of national citizenship? Of state citizenship?
   e. How have the rights of aliens been changed over time?
   f. Trace the American immigration program from the early "open door" policy through the 1924 and 1965 immigration acts.
   g. How was the 1965 immigration act a major turning point in our immigration policy?
   h. What changes were made by the 1986 immigration act?
   i. How should the U.S. government deal with undocumented aliens?

3. Property Rights/Due Process Rights/Privacy Rights
   a. How is private property protected by the contract clause?
   b. What is eminent domain?
   c. What is the difference between procedural due process and substantive due process?
   d. How do you explain the fact that substantive due process is no longer a serious check on legislative regulation of economic matters?
   e. What are the legal tender and contract clauses?
   f. What constitutional basis is used today to expand the right to privacy?
   g. What rights to abortion were given to women by *Roe v. Wade?*
   h. How does the Supreme Court view sexual orientation rights?
   i. What are the key provisions of the USA Patriot Act of 2001?

4. Rights of Persons Accused of Crime
   a. Under what restrictions do the police operate in making searches, arrests, and using deadly force?
   b. What controversy surrounds the exclusionary rule?
   c. What is the source of these rights: 1) to remain silent; 2) third-degree confessions? What is the significance of a grant of immunity?
   d. What protection is provided to a person accused of a crime by the Fourth, Fifth, Sixth and Eighth Amendments?

e. What are the procedures involved in gaining a fair trial, indictments, and sentencing/punishment?

f. What restrictions on capital punishment have been imposed by the Court?

g. Which criticisms are directed at the "three strikes and you're out" principle?

h. What is meant by double jeopardy?

i. What controversies surround terrorists and the use of military tribunals?

5. How Just Is Our System of Justice?/The Supreme Court and Civil Liberties

a. What arguments are advanced to prove that our system is just? Unjust?

b. Why do some people believe that our justice system discriminates against ethnic and racial minorities? Also, why is there controversy surrounding the jury system?

c. Ultimately, on what is our guarantee of freedom and liberty based?

d. How does community policing work?

e. Why are there objections to "racial profiling"?

f. What is the relationship between the Supreme Court and civil liberties?

g. What is the relationship between liberty and doctor-assisted suicide?

PART II — PRETEST

1. Rules and regulations that restrain those in government exercise power is referred to as
   a. police powers.
   b. expatriation rights.
   c. immunity rights.
   d. due process.

2. Current immigration law
   a. can deport legally admitted aliens if they commit crimes.
   b. is based on the prefrerential norm of "family reunification."
   c. does permit political refugees to be admitted.
   d. all of the above

3. All of the following are exceptions to the general rule against warrantless searches/seizures except:
   a. the plain-view exception.
   b. exigent circumstances.
   c. the "automobile" exception.
   d. the "residence" exception.

4. Persons who are arrested by federal officers at the scene of a crime are presumed to be
   a. guilty.
   b. innocent.
   c. accomplices.
   d. suspect.

5. Federally guaranteed rights include all of the following except
   a. no double jeopardy.
   b. right to counsel.
   c. excessive fines and unusual punishments.
   d. parole and/or probation.

6. The concept that private property cannot be taken for public use without just compensation is
   a. eminent domain.
   b. habeas corpus.
   c. *ex post facto* law.
   d. martial law.

7. Protection against self-incrimination should prevent
    a. double jeopardy.
    b. habeas corpus.
    c. eminent domain.
    d. police brutality.

8. Aliens do not have the right to
    a. jury trial.
    b. freedom of religion.
    c. vote.
    d. attend school.

9. A true bill or indictment is associated with
    a. a petit jury.
    b. plea bargaining.
    c. eminent domain.
    d. a grand jury.

10. Substantive due process today is primarily concerned with
    a. property rights.
    b. social policy.
    c. civil liberties.
    d. economic regulation.

PART III — PROGRAMMED REVIEW

Knowledge Objective: To review our Constitutional Rights to life, liberty, and property
1. _____ _____ is the established rules and regulations that restrain those in government who exercise power.
2. _____ is the legal action conferring citizenship upon an alien.
3. An applicant for naturalization must be _____ years of age.

Knowledge Objective: To analyze how the Constitution protects citizenship
4. Citizenship was given constitutional protection in 1868 with the adoption of the _____ Amendment.
5. Dual citizenshiip for Americans grows by _____ per year.
6. The right of individuals to renounce their citizenship is the _____ of _____..
7. The immigration law of 1986 attempted to deal with _____ aliens.
8. There are currently _____ to _____ million undocumented aliens (estimated).
9. Millions of illegal aliens have entered the United States from _____.

Knowledge Objective: To examine constitutional protections of property
10. The USA Patriot Act authorizes _____ wiretaps, or wiretaps on any telephone used by a person suspected of terrorism.
11. The due process of law clause is contained in both the _____ and _____ Amendments.
12. There are two kinds of due process, _____ and _____.
13. Procedural due process (does, does not) _____ apply to many methods of law enforcement.
14. The unrestricted right of women to have an abortion during the first trimester of pregnancy is an example of _____ due process.
15. The Supreme Court (has, has not) _____ ruled that state employees are entitled to due process hearings before being fired.
16. A stop and frisk exception to searches (was, was not) _____ upheld by the Supreme Court in 1968.

17. State laws that prohibit homosexual acts in private homes have been (upheld, struck down) _____ by the Supreme Court.
18. _____ due process places limits on how governmental power may be exercised.
19. _____ due process places limits on why governmental power may be exercised.
20. Substantive due process deals with the _____ of the law.

Knowledge Objective: To inquire into arbitrary arrest, questioning, and imprisonment

21. Officers (may, may not) _____ stop and search suspects if they have reason to believe they are armed and dangerous.
22. A search warrant must describe what places are to be _____ and the things that are to be _____.
23. In *Mapp v. Ohio*, the Supreme Court ruled that evidence obtained unconstitutionally (can, cannot) _____ be used in a criminal trial.
24. Witnesses before a Congressional committee may not refuse to testify if they have been granted _____.
25. Critics of the exclusionary rule argue that the solution is to punish the (police, suspect) _____.
26. In *Miranda v. Arizona,* the Supreme Court held that a conviction (could, could not) _____ stand if evidence introduced at the trial was a result of "custodial interrogation."
27. President Bush declared that foreign terrorists were to be classified as enemy _____.
28. Double jeopardy prevents two criminal trials by the _____ government for the same _____ offense.

Knowledge Objective: To evaluate our system of justice

29. Critics who claim our justice system is unreliable often point to trial by _____ as the chief source of trouble.
30. The targeting of racial minorities as potential suspects is called _____ _____.
31. Many members of minorities (do, do not)_____ think that they have equal protection under the law.
32. In the United States, our emphasis on judicial protection of civil liberties focuses attention on the _____ _____.
33. In the 1990s states have chosen to re-write jury system laws to counter the effects of _____.
34. Programs to move police from patrol cars into neighborhoods and to work with groups in society is called _____ _____.
35. Double jeopardy protections may not prevent a defendant from being subjected to both _____ and _____ trials.

PART IV — POST-TEST

1. To become a citizen of the United States, aliens have to do all of the following things except
   a. renounce allegiance to their native country.
   b. swear that they will bear arms for the U.S.
   c. swear to defend the Constitution.
   d. own property worth at least $2,000.

2. Naturalized citizens are not required to demonstrate that they
   a. are of good moral character.

b. are able to speak and write English.

c. know the principles of U.S. government.

d. have a sponsoring family.

3. In its efforts to block the entry of illegal aliens, the Naturalization Service has been
   a. moderately successful.
   b. unsuccessful.
   c. extremely successful.
   d. uninvolved.

4. Under *Roe v. Wade* the Court held that a woman in her first three months of pregnancy had a(n) _____ right to abortion.
   a. no
   b. limited
   c. court approved
   d. unrestricted

5. In 2002, which state passed a bill giving homosexual couples the same rights and benefits as married heterosexuals?
   a. Oregon
   b. Massachusetts
   c. California
   d. Pennsylvania

6. A criminal who pleads guilty to an offense that is lesser than the one with which he had been charged is said to have engaged in
   a. the exclusionary process.
   b. self-incrimination.
   c. plea bargaining.
   d. double jeopardy.

7. What element(s) must be present for the "exclusionary rule", which provides that certain evidence cannot be used to convict a person in a criminal trial, to be applicable?
   a. employees against employers
   b. children against parents
   c. illegal police searches
   d. testimony given in exchange for immunity

8. As a result of the Miranda decision, all persons accused of a crime have the following rights except
   a. to remain silent.
   b. have a lawyer represent them.
   c. freedom on bail.
   d. halt their interrogation any point.

9. In the 1990s, the Rehnquist Court made it easier to do all of the following except
   a. cut back on appeals.
   b. impose death sentences.
   c. carry out executions.
   d. appeal a plea bargain.

10. In the last decade, the number of death row inmates have
    a. increased slightly.
    b. decreased slightly.
    c. increased dramatically.
    d. decreased dramatically.

PART V — TEST ANSWERS

Pretest

1.	d	6.	a
2.	a	7.	d
3.	d	8.	c
4.	b	9.	d
5.	c	10.	c

Programmed Review

1. Due process
2. Naturalization
3. Over 18
4. Fourteenth
5. 50,000
6. right of expatriation
7. undocumented
8. 2.3; 2.4
9. Mexico
10. roving
11. Fifth; Fourteenth
12. procedural; substantive
13. does
14. substantive
15. has
16. was
17. upheld
18. procedural
19. Substantive
20. content
21. may
22. searched; seized
23. cannot
24. immunity
25. police
26. could not
27. combatants
28. same; criminal
29. jury
30. racial profiling
31. do not
32. Supreme Court
33. nullification
34. community policing
35. civil, criminal

Post-test

1.	d	6.	c
2.	d	7.	c
3.	b	8.	c
4.	d	9.	d
5.	d	10.	c

Chapter 18
Equal Rights Under the Law

PART I — GUIDEPOSTS

1. Introduction/Equality and Equal Rights/The Quest for Equal Justice
   a. What are the different concepts of equality? What are natural rights? What do the terms "civil rights" and "civil liberties" mean?
   b. Trace the struggle of women/blacks to secure the suffrage and equal rights.
   c. Why did the Civil War amendments fail to give blacks equality?
   d. Why did the federal government become involved in African-American protests in the 1960s? Also, why were affirmative action programs started?
   e. What forms of pressure did African Americans use in their struggle for equality? Why was the Civil Rights Act of 1964 so important? Who were Martin Luther King Jr. and Rosa Parks, and why were they important to the struggle?
   f. What was the conclusion of the Kerner Commission?
   g. Why was the demand by Native Americans for equal rights so long delayed?
   h. Why is the political power of Hispanics growing?
   i. How are Asian-American demands for equality fragmented? What is the social/political/economic status of Chinese, Japanese, and Vietnamese Americans?
   j. Characterize the political, social, and economic status of Native Americans.

2. What Does Equal Protection of the Laws Mean?
   a. What are the rational basis, suspect classifications, and strict scrutiny tests?
   b. Differentiate between suspect and quasi-suspect classifications of groups.
   c. Are age and poverty proper classifications?
   d. List fundamental rights of Americans. What rights are not fundamental?
   e. What essential criteria prove that a law is discriminatory?

3. Voting Rights
   a. What devices were used by Southern states to circumvent the Fourteenth and Fifteenth Amendments?
   b. How were these devices curbed by the Voting Rights Act of 1965?
   c. What changes in political life did the 1965 law bring?
   d. What constitutes diluting of minority voting power? What are "majority-minority" congressional districts?

4. Education Rights
   a. Why was the Court's decision in *Plessy v. Ferguson* so significant?
   b. In what fundamental way was the *Plessy* decision reversed by *Brown v. Board of Education?* What are *de jure* and *de facto* segregation?
   c. How does affirmative action affect school programs and activities?
   d. What conflicting forces have been involved in school busing?

103

5. Rights of Association, Accommodations, Jobs and Homes
   a. Upon what constitutional basis did Congress justify laws against discrimination?
   b. What national impact did the 1964 Civil Rights Act have on employment? (Title VII and EEOC) and Public Accommodations (Title II)?
   c. Why has housing legislation against discrimination been less successful? What were restrictive covenants?

6. Affirmative Action: Is it Constitutional?/Equal Rights Today
   a. Is affirmative action constitutional? What was Proposition 209? What was Initiative 200?
   b. What was the significance of the *Bakke* case? What is reverse discrimination?
   c. What fundamental conflict lies at the base of the affirmative action issue? Review the Shaw-Jones text debate on the pros/cons of affirmative action.
   d. Why is the plight of the "underclass" still an important issue?

PART II — PRETEST

1. Since 1960 the women's movement has not concentrated on
   a. pay.
   b. pensions.
   c. parenthood.
   d. peace.

2. The "boat people" refugees applied to which minority group?
   a. Chicanos
   b. Puerto Ricans
   c. Asian Americans
   d. African Americans

3. The civil rights gains of the 1960s chiefly benefited
   a. young black males.
   b. black welfare mothers.
   c. the black middle class.
   d. poverty stricken blacks.

4. Half of all Hispanic Americans live in the two U.S. states of
   a. California and Texas.
   b. Florida and New Mexico.
   c. New York and Louisiana.
   d. Michigan and Arizona.

5. A state legislature may classify people only if the classification meets a _____ test.
   a. suspect
   b. almost suspect
   c. fundamental rights
   d. rational basis

6. The 1896 Supreme Court ruling that approved of "separate but equal" was
   a. *Brown v. Board of Education.*
   b. *Roe v. Wade.*
   c. *Plessy v. Ferguson.*
   d. *Dred Scott.*

7. One of the following is unconstitutional as an age classification.
   a. Driver licenses may not be issued to those under 16.
   b. Alcohol may not be sold to those persons under 21.

c. A state policeman is retired at age 55.

d. An applicant for a teaching position (age 57) is rejected on the basis of age.

8. Slavery was abolished and African Americans' equal rights were granted by the _____ Amendments.
   a. Eighteenth, Nineteenth, and Twentieth
   b. Thirteenth, Fourteenth, and Fifteenth
   c. Sixteenth, Seventeenth, and Eighteenth
   d. Twelfth and Sixteenth

9. In the 1930s, African Americans resorted to which of these strategies to secure their rights?
   a. violence
   b. political power
   c. litigation
   d. persuasion

10. The civil rights movement produced its first charismatic leader during the Montgomery, Alabama, bus boycott of 1955.
    a. James Baldwin
    b. Dick Gregory
    c. Martin Luther King Jr.
    d. Jesse Jackson

PART III — PROGRAMMED REVIEW

Knowledge Objective: To examine the role of government in providing equal rights

1. Most Americans do not accept the equality of (opportunity, results) _____.
2. Affirmative action is designed to help people disadvantaged by their _____ memberships.
3. The focus of the modern women's rights movement has been to secure adoption of the _____ _____ Amendment.
4. A major handicap of the Hispanics has been their _____ which is not mainstream America.
5. Hispanics were courted by both presidential candidates in the year _____.
6. A 1988 law provided $20,000 as restitution to _____-_____ interned during World War II.
7. Native Americans are a separate people with power to regulate their own internal affairs, subject to _____ supervision.
8. After the Civil War, three "civil rights" amendments were added to the Constitution, the _____, _____ and _____ Amendments.
9. The first branch of the national government to become sensitized to the aspirations of African Americans was the _____.
10. In the 1930s, blacks resorted to _____ to secure their rights.
11. In the 1960s, the use of litigation by blacks was supplemented by a widespread _____, _____ and _____ movement.
12. The immediate origin of the black revolt occurred in 1955 when a _____ boycott was organized in Montgomery, Alabama.
13. A U.S. Civil Rights commission found that Asian Americans (do, do not) _____ face widespread discrimination.

Knowledge Objective: To examine equal protection under the laws

14. The equal protection of the laws clause is part of the _____ Amendment and is implied in the due process clause of the _____ Amendment.
15. The Constitution forbids only _____ classification.
16. The traditional test of whether a law complies with the equal protection requirement is the _____ basis test.
17. Race and national origins are obviously _____ classifications.
18. The quasi-suspect classification includes _____ and _____.
19. More than a generation after the Kerner Report, life for inner-city minorities is _____.
20. Poverty, according to the Supreme Court, (is, is not) _____ an unconstitutional classification.
21. Age (can, cannot) _____ be used as a criterion in employment if it is related to proper job performance.

Knowledge Objective: To describe the life and death of Jim Crow in Education

22. In the 1954 case of _____ v. _____ the Supreme Court reversed its 1896 decision in *Plessy v. Ferguson*.
23. Segregation required by law is called _____ _____ segregation.
24. When segregation occurs without sanction of law, it is called _____ _____ segregation.
25. Busing across school district lines (is, is not) _____ required if the school district lines have been drawn to maintain segregation.

Knowledge Objective: To review barriers to voting

26. Most suffrage requirements, inside the U.S. constitutional framework, are fixed by the _____.
27. The Voting Rights Act of 1965 has been (effective, ineffective) _____.
28. The poll tax was abolished in federal elections by the _____ Amendment.
29. The Voting Rights Act of 1965 as amended set aside _____ tests throughout the country.
30. In attempting to give minorities a majority district, the result will probably be more minority districts and more safe _____ districts.
31. In _____ v. _____ the Supreme Court ruled that race cannot be the sole reason for drawing voting district lines.

Knowledge Objective: To examine racial and sexual barriers to public accommodations, jobs, and homes

32. The Fourteenth Amendment applies only to _____ action and not to private groups serving only their own members.
33. Segregation in places of _____ accommodation is unconstitutional.
34. A training program that gives preference to minorities or women (is, is not) _____ constitutional.
35. The Court (upheld/struck down) _____ the Richmond, Virginia, plan to require nonminority contractors to subcontract work to minority business.

36. Attempts through legislation to end housing discrimination (have, have not) _____ been a great success.
37. In the *Bakke* case the Supreme Court held that a special admissions category from which whites were excluded was (constitutional, unconstitutional) _____.
38. To redress the discrimination suffered by minorities, governments have adopted _____ _____ programs.
39. Affirmative action programs may temporarily set _____ but not _____.
40. The adoption of California's Proposition 209 and Washington's Initiative 200 outlawed _____ _____ programs.

PART IV — POST-TEST

1. Upon passage of the Nineteenth Amendment, women
   a. received equal pay.
   b. received equal rights.
   c. put an end to legal discrimination.
   d. got the right to vote.

2. Identify the unrelated word.
   a. freedom rides
   b. sit-ins
   c. bus boycott
   d. violence

3. The Kerner Report declared that
   a. violence is as American as apple pie.
   b. our nation was moving toward two societies, separate and unequal.
   c. affirmative action is un-American.
   d. black children should have neighborhood schools.

4. The minority with the greatest voting potential is
   a. Indians.
   b. Vietnamese.
   c. Hispanics.
   d. African Americans.

5. A reasonable government classification would be based on
   a. age.
   b. religion.
   c. sex.
   d. race.

6. Since 1960 the national government's role in the issue of equal rights has been to
   a. support discrimination.
   b. remain neutral.
   c. take affirmative action.
   d. defer to the states.

7. One of the following situations is outside government jurisdiction.
   a. a restaurant bars men without jacket and tie
   b. a hotel refuses to register a rock-and-roll star
   c. a realtor refuses to sell property to an extended Vietnamese family
   d. a theater refuses to seat a group with long hair and blue jeans

8. _____ is a fundamental right.
   a. Travel
   c. Welfare

b. Housing   d. Education

9. Which of these cases marked the end of the separate but equal interpretation of the Constitution?
   a. *Plessy v. Ferguson*   c. *Bakke v. California Regents*
   b. *Weber v. Kaiser*   d. *Brown v. Board of Education*

10. After the 2000 election, which group complained that they were discouraged from voting or their votes were not counted in Florida?
    a. Asian Americans   c. Hispanics
    b. African Americans   d. all of the above

PART V — TEST ANSWERS

Pretest

1.	c	6.	c
2.	c	7.	d
3.	d	8.	b
4.	a	9.	c
5.	d	10.	c

Programmed Review

1. results
2. Group
3. Equal Rights
4. Language
5. 2000
6. Japanese-Americans
7. Congressional
8. Thirteenth; Fourteenth; Fifteenth
9. executive
10. litigation
11. social; economic; political
12. bus
13. do
14. Fourteenth; Fifth
15. unreasonable
16. rational
17. suspect
18. sex; illegitimacy
19. worse
20. is not

21. can
22. *Brown v. Board of Education*
23. de jure
24. de facto
25. is
26. states
27. effective
28. Twenty-Fourth
29. literacy
30. Republican
31. Shaw, Reno
32. government
33. public
34. is
35. struck down
36. have not
37. unconstitutional
38. affirmative action
39. goals, quotas
40. affirmative action

Post-test

1. d
2. d
3. b
4. c
5. a

6. c
7. a
8. a
9. d
10. b

Chapter 19
The Democratic Faith

PART I — GUIDEPOSTS

1. Introduction/The Case for Government by the People
    a. Why is an "active, committed citizenry" in the U.S. so important? What do the "Voices on the Democratic Faith" reveal about democratic values?
    b. Why is it important to achieve a balance between liberty and societal needs?
    c. What competing social and political values confront Americans?
    d. What components of democratic government were blended in our Constitution?
    e. How did the Founders value efficient government as contrasted with safe government?
        What did the Framers learn from the rise and decline of ancient Athens?
    f. How did the spirit of the "American community" manifest itself after the terrorist attacks of 9/11?

2. Participation and Representation
    a. What problems exist in participatory government?
    b. How are these problems lessened by representative government? How can direct participation help through its two concomitant purposes?
    c. How does congressional representation reduce majority rule as reflected by the president? What is *Duverger's law*?
    d. What is broker rule? Do we have it? Why is the U.S. system so "considerate of dissent and criticism"? Why is the trend toward direct democracy likely to continue?
    e. Why do Americans have a love-hate relationship with politicians?
    f. Describe the gap between our idealized politician and reality.
    g. Why are politicians necessary to make democracy work? What does the oath "Proud to be a Politician" reveal about the political process?

3. Reconciling Democracy and Leadership
    a. Why is there no freedom without politics? Why do people run for office? Why are people reluctant to run for office?
    b. How do leaders differ from managers?
    c. Why is the "ultimate test of a democratic system the legal existence of an officially recognized opposition"?

4. The Democratic Faith
    a. What elements constituted the democratic faith for Thomas Jefferson?
    b. What relationship exists among democracy, education, and information?
    c. According to historian Arthur M. Schlesinger, what is the "genius of America"?
    d. What is important about the fact that "people can fight city hall" in America?

PART II — PRETEST

1. The "ultimate test" of a democratic system is the legal existence of a
   - a. competitive party system.
   - b. free educational system.
   - c. free market.
   - d. recognized opposition.

2. American politicians tend to win their great acclaim
   - a. shortly after election.
   - b. while running for office.
   - c. after death.
   - d. when they win reelection.

3. Critics of broker rule believe all of the following except
   - a. election laws are too complicated.
   - b. low income persons are less heard.
   - c. parties do not offer meaningful alternatives.
   - d. a bias exists for the status quo.

4. At the very heart of those personal characteristics that motivate politicians is
   - a. ideology.
   - b. ambition.
   - c. selfishness.
   - d. craftiness.

5. A Greek spokesman who declared that government was everyone's business is
   - a. Socrates.
   - b. Pericles.
   - c. Zorba.
   - d. Heroditus.

6. The most important element in American government today is
   - a. interest groups.
   - b. committed citizens.
   - c. great leaders.
   - d. obedient followers.

7. Direct participation in decision making
   - a. will enhance the dignity of the individuals involved.
   - b. will act as a safeguard against dictatorship.
   - c. rests on a theory of self-protection.
   - d. all of the above

8. Direct democracy works best when
   - a. an area is small.
   - b. a society is pluralistic.
   - c. people are well educated.
   - d. standards of living are high.

9. Participatory democracy works best in
   - a. neighborhood associations.
   - b. cities.
   - c. states.
   - d. the armed forces.

10. Broker rule is best described as
    - a. compromises between conflicting groups.
    - b. substituting interest groups for parties.
    - c. regulation by the New York Stock Exchange.

d. giving women greater power.

PART III — PROGRAMMED REVIEW

Knowledge Objective: To analyze the Democratic Faith
1. According to democratic theory, the only legitimate foundation for any government is the _____ of the people.
2. The democratic concept in practice is a mixture of _____ and _____.
3. In the full span of human history, most people have lived under _____ rule.
4. Freedom and _____ go together.
5. As Athens declined, Athenians wanted _____ more than liberty or freedom.
6. Leadership is important in a democracy, but even more important is an _____ citizenry.
7. The American community came together after the _____ attacks of 9/11.

Knowledge Objective: To review the basic guiding principles of American democratic government
8.   _____ was the principle most valued by the framers.
9. The Constitution both _____ and _____ power to national, state, and local governments.
10. The Constitution distributes power between the _____ and _____ governments.
11. Efficiency (was, was not) _____ the main goal of the framers.
12. The framers tried to protect individual liberty _____ government.
13. The framers wanted to make government responsive to the people but to insulate it from momentary _____.

Knowledge Objective: To examine the prospects for American democratic government
14. Individual needs and the needs of society must be _____.
15. Negotiations between interest groups within the Congress that result in compromise legislation is called _____ rule.
16. Democratic governments always have _____ groups that are free to speak out.

Knowledge Objective: To analyze American attitudes toward politicians
17. American citizens (are, are not) _____ normally critical of their government.
18. Leadership can be understood only in the context of both leaders and _____.
19. Politicians are held in _____ (low, high) public esteem.
20. Our ideal leaders are usually _____ (dead, alive).
21. We probably expect too (much, little) _____ of politicians.

Knowledge Objective: To define the various kinds of leadership
22. A leader without _____ is a contradiction in terms.
23. As political brokers, the coalition builders try to work out _____ between divergent groups.
24. _____ is the lifeblood of democracy.
25. Our political system depends on people willing to compete for _____.
26. Managers and leaders (do, do not) _____ require the same skills.

27. One reason why people run for office is to satisfy _____ needs.
28. There (is, is not) _____ a single effective style that all leaders should learn and practice.
29. One reason why people do not run for office is due to a loss of _____.

Knowledge Objective: To review the Democratic Faith
30. _____ is one of the best predictors of voting.
31. Thomas Jefferson believed there is nothing in the country that cannot be cured by good _____ and sound _____ _____.
32. Our political system is far from perfect, but it is still an _____ system.

PART IV — POST-TEST

1. The principal objective of the framers was
   a. efficient government.
   b. representative government.
   c. individual liberty.
   d. responsive representatives.

2. The virtues of our present political system include
   a. easy leadership.
   b. safeguards against tyranny.
   c. decisive action.
   d. quick response to majorities.

3. The framers were least interested in making the government
   a. moderate.
   b. balanced.
   c. safe.
   d. efficient.

4. In the last days of Athenian democracy, the most common aspiration was for
   a. liberty.
   b. freedom.
   c. security.
   d. equality.

5. One of the greatest spokesmen for an educated citizenry was
   a. Alexander Hamilton.
   b. John Adams.
   c. Warren Harding.
   d. Thomas Jefferson.

6. The full operation of majority rule is slowed by all of the following *except*
   a. federalism.
   b. free elections.
   c. Bill of Rights.
   d. checks and balances.

7. People are reluctant to run for public office due to
   a. media criticism.
   b. campaign expenses.
   c. fear of compromising principles.
   d. all of the above.

8. In writing the Constitution, all of the following goals were sought *except*
   a. a government that would work.
   b. individual liberty.
   c. responsive government.
   d. preservation of strong local governments.

9. Crucial to the democratic faith is the belief that a constitutional democracy cherishes
   a. rule by force.
   c. the free play of ideas.
   b. majority rule.
   d. rule by the better and the wise.

10. People run for political office in order to
    a. advance fresh ideas.
    c. to gain prominence and power.
    b. gain a voice in policy-making.
    d. all of the above

PART V — TEST ANSWERS

Pre-test

1.	d	6.	b
2.	c	7.	d
3.	a	8.	a
4.	b	9.	a
5.	b	10.	a

Programmed Review

1.	will	17.	are
2.	**faith; skepticism**	**18.**	**followers**
3.	authoritarian	19.	low
4.	obligation	20.	dead
5.	security	21.	much
6.	active	22.	power
7.	terrorist	23.	compromises
8.	Liberty	24.	Politics
9.	grants; withholds	25.	office
10.	**national; state**	**26.**	**do not**
11.	was not	27.	ego
12.	against	28.	is not
13.	majorities	29.	privacy
14.	balanced	30.	education
15.	broker	31.	newspapers, school masters
16.	minority or opposition	32.	open

Post-test

1.	c	6.	b
2.	b	7.	d
3.	d	8.	d
4.	**c**	**9.**	**c**
5.	d	10.	d